A New Look at Successful Programs

PROPERTY OF
COMMUNICATION SKILLS CENTER
OHIO NORTHERN UNIVERSITY.

John E. Roueche, *Editor*

NEW DIRECTIONS FOR COLLEGE LEARNING ASSISTANCE
KURT V. LAURIDSEN, *Editor-in-Chief*

Number 11, March 1983

Paperback sourcebooks in
The Jossey-Bass Higher Education Series

Jossey-Bass Inc., Publishers
San Francisco • Washington • London

John E. Roueche (Ed.).
A New Look at Successful Programs.
New Directions for College Learning Assistance.
San Francisco: Jossey-Bass, 1983.

New Directions for College Learning Assistance Series
Kurt V. Lauridsen, *Editor-in-Chief*

Copyright © 1983 by Jossey-Bass Inc., Publishers
and
Jossey-Bass Limited

Copyright under International, Pan American, and Universal
Copyright Conventions. All rights reserved. No part of
this issue may be reproduced in any form—except for brief
quotation (not to exceed 500 words) in a review or professional
work—without permission in writing from the publishers.

New Directions for College Learning Assistance is published quarterly
by Jossey-Bass Inc., Publishers. Subscriptions, single-issue orders,
change of address notices, undelivered copies, and other
correspondence should be sent to *New Directions* Subscriptions,
Jossey-Bass Inc., Publishers, 433 California Street, San Francisco,
California 94104.

Editorial correspondence should be sent to the Editor-in-Chief,
Kurt V. Lauridsen, Director, Student Learning Center,
University of California, Berkeley, California 94720.

Library of Congress Catalogue Card Number LC 82-84176

International Standard Serial Number ISSN 0271-0617

International Standard Book Number ISBN 87589-935-8

Cover art by Willi Baum

Manufactured in the United States of America

Ordering Information

The paperback sourcebooks listed below are published quarterly and can be ordered either by subscription or single-copy.

Subscriptions cost $35.00 per year for institutions, agencies, and libraries. Individuals can subscribe at the special rate of $21.00 per year *if payment is by personal check*. (Note that the full rate of $35.00 applies if payment is by institutional check, even if the subscription is designated for an individual.) Standing orders are accepted. Subscriptions normally begin with the first of the four sourcebooks in the current publication year of the series. When ordering, please indicate if you prefer your subscription to begin with the first issue of the *coming* year.

Single copies are available at $7.95 when payment accompanies order, and *all single-copy orders under $25.00 must include payment*. (California, New Jersey, New York, and Washington, D.C., residents please include appropriate sales tax.) For billed orders, cost per copy is $7.95 plus postage and handling. (Prices subject to change without notice.)

Bulk orders (ten or more copies) of any individual sourcebook are available at the following discounted prices: 10–49 copies, $7.15 each; 50–100 copies, $6.35 each; over 100 copies, *inquire*. Sales tax and postage and handling charges apply as for single copy orders.

To ensure correct and prompt delivery, all orders must give either the *name of an individual* or an *official purchase order number*. Please submit your order as follows:

Subscriptions: specify series and year subscription is to begin.
Single Copies: specify sourcebook code (such as, CLA8) and first two words of title.

Mail orders for United States and Possessions, Latin America, Canada, Japan, Australia, and New Zealand to:
Jossey-Bass Inc., Publishers
433 California Street
San Francisco, California 94104

Mail orders for all other parts of the world to:
Jossey-Bass Limited
28 Banner Street
London EC1Y 8QE

New Directions for College Learning Assistance Series
Kurt V. Lauridsen, *Editor-in-Chief*

Contents

Editor's Notes

Formal evaluation of programs for low-achieving students by American colleges and universities is still rare. In fact, most collegiate programs are not characterized by written statements of rationale, design, or intended outcomes. The reader should not infer from this, however, that evaluation of educational programs is commonplace in other curriculum areas, for evaluation is neither typical nor usual in education. Because colleges and universities are now being forced to accept thousands of high school graduates each year who cannot read, write, speak, listen, study, or figure well enough to enroll in regular freshman-level college courses, formal evaluation of remedial and compensatory programs becomes imperative if colleges are to retain the public moral and financial support that is necessary if they are to continue offering such courses and services to students who cannot succeed without them.

Thankfully, a few colleges, universities, and individuals have examined the impact of some programs and strategies intended for use with low-achieving students. These studies conclude that well-conceived developmental programs can improve achievement levels so that skill-deficient students can expect to survive and succeed in college. They also show that such programs can be cost-effective as well. This volume reports on these studies and spotlights services and strategies that have proved effective in developing students' academic skills and attributes to levels needed for success in college.

In Chapter One, Suanne D. Roueche reviews a recent University of Texas study of college responses to low-achieving students. She pays special attention to common program elements found in the nation's most successful programs. In Chapter Two, Lee Noel and Diana Saluri maintain that colleges and curricular programs must focus on learning outcomes as the proper goal for educational institutions. They report on a recent study of college programs designed to achieve predetermined outcomes. In Chapter Three, Susan S. Obler reviews recent studies and reports of successful college programs for high-risk learners. She summarizes findings and recommendations and cites five critical areas of concern for program designers. In Chapter Four, Lynn B. Burnham reports on her recent investigation of successful developmental programs in Texas. She finds that teacher behaviors in the classroom are the critical factors associated with student success.

In Chapter Five, Phoebe K. Helm and Sunil Chand describe the developmental education program at Triton College and share results of their efforts to improve student persistence and achievement. The philosophy and program offerings of the University of Wisconsin–Parkside collegiate skills program are described by Carol J. Cashen in Chapter Six. Program outcomes are well documented in this chapter. Robert E. Glennen, president of West-

1

tern New Mexico University, discusses the rationale and results of his institution's intrusive advising programs in Chapter Seven. One outcome of that university's strategy is improved student persistence in college. In Chapter Eight, George Baker and Percy Painter establish criteria for management of effective learning centers and describe the center at Sumter Area Technical College, which shows what can be accomplished when all components are in place and strong leadership provides the coherence necessary for program accountability. In Chapter Nine, Mary Stubbs demonstrates how careful program evaluation and documentation of costs can help to foster acceptance and support by college colleagues and staff. Finally, Lynn B. Burnham provides an annotated bibliography of reports and studies of programs that emphasize program outcomes. This list will be of particular value to those who wish to evaluate program results.

All these authors, as well as other researchers, show that most college students today possess the aptitudes and abilities that they need in order to succeed in college. The major problem that students bring to campus is one of not having been taught very well. Many of today's students have matriculated from high schools that gave them little experience in reading, writing, or studying. They have not been required to do homework, written assignments are almost nonexistent, and essay examinations are relics of an era in American education when pride in teaching excellence was common. However, even these students can learn and be successful both in school and in later life if institutions build programs that require them to learn. Academic skills can be developed only by serious engagement in the activity in which they are required. There is no shortcut or easy path to high levels of student proficiency. Colleges must make a serious effort to describe and document their program efforts and results with low-achieving students.

John E. Roueche
Editor

John E. Roueche is professor and director at the Program in Community College Education, The University of Texas at Austin. He has conducted five national investigations of college remedial programs since 1968.

*A new national study of college and university responses
to low-achieving students concludes that discussions about basic skill
development have turned from* should *to* how *these efforts can be
made in higher educational settings.*

Elements of Program Success:
Report of a National Study

Suanne D. Roueche

As institutions of higher education face increasing numbers of students who
cannot read, write, or figure at acceptable levels, it becomes increasingly
important to maintain some ongoing sense of institutional responses to these
low-achieving students. And, because *low-achieving* no longer describes only
the academically poor or nontraditional student but also the traditionally prepared and presumably academically successful student, it is necessary to poll
all colleges and universities about the plight of all institutions of higher education. For, at the present time, community colleges no longer have the singular
distinction of facing these increasing numbers of underprepared students.
Even the most selective institutions are joining them as some of the "best" students that colleges and universities enroll demonstrate unconscionably low levels of even the most basic skills.

An Expanding Problem

While more selective institutions may not choose to provide basic skill
development services to increasingly greater numbers of entering students, the
sheer magnitude of the nation's problem guarantees that they will not be
spared this dilemma, which seems to recognize no former social or educational
privileges. For their own economic well-being, colleges and universities must

J. E. Roueche (Ed.). *A New Look at Successful Programs.* New Directions
for College Learning Assistance, no. 11. San Francisco: Jossey-Bass, March 1983.

develop and implement responsible ways of providing such skill development. To turn away students who cannot meet traditional institutional entrance requirements or students who demonstrate gaps between their academic preparation and the expectations and demands that education makes of them would reduce enrollment severely and endanger the life of the institution. Colleges and universities must attempt to save these entering students — that is, to bring their skills to acceptable levels for successful work — in order to keep the students in school and thereby save themselves economically. Colleges and universities must also educate students to meet the increasingly complex demands of the real world. If institutions choose to ignore the literacy problem — turning away low-achieving students for want of a skill development program; enrolling such students conditionally, perhaps in the hope that they will somehow improve; moving low-achieving students through courses that do not require them to demonstrate acceptable levels of skill development; or merely allowing them to fail in courses for which they are unprepared — the projected literacy dilemma will worsen beyond all present expectations.

A National Study

During the spring and summer of 1982, the University of Texas conducted a national study of college and university responses to low-achieving students. This study was the first of its kind. All colleges and universities on the American Council of Education's list of senior institutions and all community, junior, and technical colleges listed in the 1981 directory of the American Association of Community/Junior Colleges received the questionnaire. We decided to disregard responses from specialized vocational and training institutions and concentrate on institutions that awarded traditional associate, baccalaureate, and graduate degrees.

Of the 2,508 surveys mailed, 1,489 were returned. Of the 1,452 usable responses, only 160 institutions reported that they did not operate basic skills programs, courses, or alternatives for meeting the needs of low-achieving students. Some of these institutions have been mentioned in articles about existing developmental efforts, or their faculties or staffs have stated publicly that the instituitons were aware of and concerned about the pervasive national literacy problem among entering students. We have no idea why these institutions chose to respond as they did. This finding, while not a surprise, confirmed the problem that we were researching. No institutions are escaping the growing literacy problem. Discussion is rapidly moving away from whether basic skills development should be offered at the college and university level, and toward how skills development should be designed and administered.

Survey questions sought to determine the magnitude of the literacy problem that colleges and universities are facing, to describe institutional efforts to develop basic skills, to determine the effectiveness of these efforts, and to identify elements of programs and courses common to institutions that reported the most positive outcomes — that is, that reported the highest retention rates for their basic skills courses and for regular courses taken after the basic skills sequence (Roueche and others, in press).

The study's attempts to identify successful programs were hampered by institutional inconsistencies in the collection and reporting of retention and other follow-up data. While we were aware that few institutions of higher education make significant efforts to evaluate courses and programs, we had hoped that the programs that have been under such scrutiny for the last two decades would be more inclined to account for themselves. Thus, we were dismayed to find that most reported retention data gave rise to the suspicion that collection procedures were not yet in place in most of the institutions that we surveyed. For the majority of responding institutions, the figures reported strongly suggested that the respondent was only making a best guess. Moreover, among the institutions that did collect retention data, the trend was toward recording program retention figures. Thus, few institutions could provide the equally important subsequent retention figures for follow-on courses.

For these reasons, we decided to identify institutions that reported 50 percent or better student retention in the basic skills courses. For the institutions in that group, we used their reported information from the survey questionnaire. We also performed some additional survey follow-up procedures — primarily efforts to determine actual enrollment and completion figures by interviewing appropriate personnel. It is from these responses and additional investigations that we inferred some elements of success. By *elements of success,* we mean elements that appear to be most predictive of success with low-achieving students and most characteristic of the reported successful basic skills development efforts.

Elements of Success

College and university basic skills development programs that reported the most complete and encouraging retention data seemed to have eleven elements in common: strong administrative support, mandatory counseling and placement, structured courses, award of credit, flexible competition strategies, multiple learning systems, volunteer instructors, use of peer tutors, monitoring of behaviors, interfacing with subsequent courses, and program evaluation.

Strong Administrative Support. There is strong administrative support for basic skills development at institutions with successful programs. Written statements appear not only in the college catalogue available to all students but in board policy manuals that support the implementation of strong assessment and placement efforts with entering students. Often, these written statements describe the institution's intent to contribute to student success. That is, the institution declares that it shares responsibility with its students for professional service in initial assessment, in placement, in early identification of poor academic performance, and in interventions designed to improve such performance, such as written plans and counseling strategies.

Mandatory Assessment and Placement. Strong administrative support is reflected in the mandatory assessment of all entering students' basic skills achievement levels and in the use of the results of such assessment to place students in appropriate basic skills courses. Students are tested before they enroll in any courses, either in preregistration or in orientation activities. Then, students are counseled about the assessment results and placed in appropriate basic skills or academic courses. Frequently, both assessment and placement are institutional conditions for enrollment. Furthermore, students must complete the required skill courses successfully before they enroll in any course that requires a higher level of skill development than they can demonstrate.

Frequently, there also are efforts to limit the number of courses in which a student may enroll. The criteria by which these scheduling decisions are made include extracurricular responsibilities, such as work and family commitments, and the nature and severity of the student's basic skills deficiencies.

Institutions with successful skills development programs report that they are no longer able to use the high school grade point average as a strong indicator of ability to negotiate college-level work. Rather, they rely on students' scores on the traditional entrance tests—ACT, SAT—as preliminary points of departure for further on-site testing. Often, the tests used for determining students' achievement levels in reading, writing, and mathematics have been produced by developmental specialists on staff, sometimes with advice from instructors of representative freshman-level courses. Typically, further testing to determine the specific levels at which basic skills development should begin is conducted once students have been assigned to skills courses.

Structured Courses. Successful basic skills developmental courses in community colleges and four-year colleges are arranged in semester-length segments. Sometimes, these courses are housed in established developmental programs. More often, they are housed in the appropriate disciplines; that is, reading and writing courses are housed in the English department, mathematics courses are housed in the mathematics department, and so forth. In the major universities, skills courses are typically housed in learning centers that serve a broad range of other institutional learning needs as well.

The common element appears to be that courses are structured; that is, they meet at scheduled days and times. There is careful monitoring of student behaviors; that is, there is individual attention to student progress, and there are strict attendance requirements. Typically, these courses use the standard marks of A, B, C, D, and F. Often, some form of nonpunitive grading—for example, a P, or progress, grade—is awarded for student progress that reflects acceptable movement toward course objectives but that does not meet productive grade-level criteria. The progress grade designates that the student is to continue in the basic skills course sequence either by re-enrolling in the same course or by enrolling in a designated second-semester course. The nonpunitive mark allows the instructor to avoid placing the student in academic jeopardy.

Award of Credit. Without exception, the successful skills development courses are credit-bearing. The credit awarded is always transcript credit, although in some instances the credit can accrue toward the fulfillment of specific degree requirements in lieu of elective courses that a student may have in a degree option.

Flexible Completion Strategies. Although typically courses are offered in semester-length segments, they are designed to accommodate the student who cannot complete the assigned work or the prescription in one semester. Thus, if the student has not met course requirements by semester's end, he can re-enroll in the skills course and begin where he left off, not at the beginning of the developmental sequence or at the course sequence level described in the college catalogue. Furthermore, at some institutions, students who can meet exit criteria or who can demonstrate the prescribed competencies or skill levels before the semester ends are allowed to leave the course at that point with the earned grade. Few courses accommodated late arrivals; that is, few courses allowed students to enter at any time during the semester. Early exit was more generally accepted. Finally, while there are variable time frames for course completion, there are predetermined, reasonable expectations for maximum time limits beyond which students must be redirected into alternative career or academic choices or simply counseled out of the institution.

Multiple Learning Systems. Successful basic skills courses use multiple learning systems and devices. Typically, students follow individual prescriptions of work prepared for them after analysis of the results of initial assessment and of in-depth, targeted, in-class assessment procedures. In these courses, instruction tends to be characterized by performance-based course objectives, self-paced modules of instruction as well as group instruction, and use of pretests and posttests to move students through their planned sequences of work. Thus, students use a variety of written and mechanical tools for progressing through assignments. Instructors cite use of multiple teaching strategies, not strict adherence to a lecture or a self-paced mode of instruction.

Student behavior is monitored, so that instructors can stay alert to problems and intervene at critical points. In most instances uncovered by the survey, a support staff of peer tutors, available to students both during classroom scheduled hours and during specified out-of-class time blocks, provided additional support for the monitoring system.

Volunteer Instructors. Instructors for these basic skills courses volunteer for their assignments. While in some instances they are chosen by a department chairperson — after they meet predetermined precurricular and instructional performance criteria or complete appropriate preparation sequences — the decision to become a candidate for the position and the decision to accept the position are the instructor's to make.

Most developmental skills faculty are full-time in their disciplines. Frequently, they teach both regular academic courses and skills courses during the same semester. Institutions provided special in-service training for these faculty members in strategies for working with low-achieving students. Typically, developmental skills faculty classroom performance is evaluated both by supervisors and by students.

While counselors are not often chosen to work especially with low-achieving students—rather, they are appointed as part of their regular work load—the counseling component is considered to be an integral part of the basic skills instructional effort. The trend in successful programs is toward individual—not group—counseling activities. Evaluation of counselors' performance is infrequent.

Use of Peer Tutors. Peer tutors are used extensively as support personnel in the classroom. In many instances, they act also as resource persons outside the organized, scheduled class sessions. Typically, peer tutors are selected on the basis of performance criteria (for example, for their solid knowledge of selected disciplines) and faculty recommendation (for example, for being attentive to detail and working well with others). They receive preservice training in working with low-achieving students, and they are evaluated regularly by supervising instructors, chairmen, and students.

Monitoring of Student Behaviors. Successful skills development courses have integral systems for the monitoring of those student behaviors that contribute to failure. These monitoring systems attend to such student behaviors as excessive absences, failure to produce assigned work, and failure to produce acceptable levels of work. Appropriate interventions include calling or writing to the student after one or more absences from class to provide assignment information that allows the student to return to class with as little interruption as possible and recycling the student through unlearned or unmastered materials.

Interfacing with Subsequent Courses. Course content and strategies for negotiating content are designed to reflect the reading, writing, and mathematical demands that subsequent courses will make on basic skills students. Basic skills faculty conduct modified needs assessments to determine not only what subsequent courses in disciplines of interest to enrolled students will require but also what generic skills and content will be important to all students, regardless of their chosen majors. Thus, there is a concerted effort to identify what is expected of the individual student after he leaves the basic skills course and to instruct toward those specific and general expectations. These efforts frequently are formalized as written exit criteria that students must meet in order to complete the basic skills course successfully.

Program Evaluation. While most responding institutions acknowledged the importance of program evaluation, few had a procedure that automatically and routinely gathered the retention data that we sought. In fact, when evaluation data are collected at all, they are still woefully inadequate to describe the outcomes of college and university efforts to respond to the increasing numbers of low-achieving students. As previously mentioned, most of the data that are collected are about basic skills program completion, not about success in subsequent academic work. This is an important distinction for evaluation of the effectiveness of developmental efforts. Furthermore, individual descriptions and interpretations of the collected data varied among personnel even within the same institution. However, the intention to increase collection efforts and to improve on current methods of evaluating program success was common among the successful progams.

A tangential outcome of plans for improving data collection procedures is development of improved retention strategies. Most of the successful programs noted that their future efforts would be directed toward researching, planning, and implementing procedures whereby students could be retained longer and with more success. Future plans described by respondents with successful skills development programs include improved preassessment strategies to identify low-achievement students prior to enrollment, more intervention strategies during the crucial first semesters to identify and counsel potential dropouts and failures, improved interfacing with subsequent courses for more refined curriculum and instructional development in the basic skills courses, and more discriminating exit interview procedures for isolating problem areas for students who fail to complete basic skills or initial subsequent academic courses.

State of the Art

The literature documents the efforts of numerous researchers whose investigations into college and university programs for low-achieving students have highlighted rather dismal outcomes. These programs are now swelling to accommodate not only those students with poor academic records but those students more traditionally regarded as the "best" and who are now demonstrating low levels of basic skill development. Institutions of higher education must move beyond haphazard programming and evaluation of these programs, since they are serving greater and greater percentages of the total institutional enrollment. It is highly probable that most institutions will be disappointed, dismayed, and depressed by the findings of their evaluation procedures. There are, however, too many forces presently at work that will not allow—indeed, that will not accept—institutional failure to meet the needs of low-achieving students. Many respondents noted that state legislators and state boards of education were threatening to reduce funding and calling for evidence that programs were in place to produce students who could be brought to acceptable academic performance levels and remain in their institutions to pursue certificates and degrees with success. Some respondents mentioned that, even without such imminent threats, the clear analysis of numbers of students unable to meet entrance requirements and students unable to complete a successful first semester, or both, indicated that some basic skills developmental intervention was no longer a subject for academic discussion but, rather, a subject for action.

The mere existence of a basic skills program will not satisfy disheartened parents and administrators or solve the economic necessity of keeping institutional doors open. Only the existence of a program that works will meet these two aims. Students must be able to demonstrate literacy skills at acceptable levels in courses required in degree fields. Instructors in academic and vocational areas should not have to require high levels of reading and writing performance from students who are incapable of it and at the same time have to attempt to retain such students while providing them with appropriate skills and content. Students should be prepared before they enroll in such courses, and they should be expected to perform at the levels that tradition has come to associate with the experience of higher education. There is dramatic evidence that this tradition is showing signs of erosion in the face of the literacy dilemma (Roueche and Comstock, 1981; Richardson and Martens, 1982).

As the results of our study indicate, the economic and educational prospects for all educational institutions leave little or no room for complacency or foot dragging. While a few institutions still will not admit that they have a literacy problem, increasing numbers are looking into the problems raised by existing responses to the literacy dilemma, into linkages that can promote the very best thinking among fledgling as well as mature program administrators and instructors about responses to low achievers, and into improving their basic skills services. Others are working to demand more of the public and private grammar and high schools that feed institutions of higher education.

Beyond the increasing numbers of organized networks for administrators and instructors of basic skills programs, national and regional conferences are regularly held to provide a forum for sharing developmental strategies. Our study shows that investigations of institutional responses to low-achieving students can make a significant contribution to attempts to deal with a problem that will not go away in the foreseeable future.

References

Richardson, R. C., Jr., and Martens, K. J. *A Report on Literacy Development in Community Colleges.* Washington, D.C.: National Institute of Education, 1982.

Roueche, J. E., Baker, G. A., and Roueche, S. D. *College Responses to Low-Achieving Students: A National Study.* New York: HBJ–Media Systems Corporation, in press.

Roueche, S. D., and Comstock, V. N. *A Report on Theory and Method for the Study of Literacy Development in Community Colleges.* Washington, D.C.: National Institute of Education, 1981.

Suanne D. Roueche is a lecturer in the Department of Educational Administration, Program in Community College Education, at the University of Texas at Austin. She directed a three-year literacy study for the National Institute of Education between 1979 and 1981, and she was researcher for the national study described in this chapter.

Serious attention to documentation of results by setting and assessing
learning outcomes is imperative in efforts to revitalize confidence
in higher education today.

Setting and Assessing
Outcomes: A Fresh Approach

Lee Noel
Diana Saluri

On many campuses across the country today, the term *general education* serves
as label for a broad array of academic offerings. The objectives of these offerings are, however, remarkably consistent. As a result of participating in the
general education endeavor, students are expected to gain competence to
function effectively in society after graduation. Unfortunately, little is known
about how successful existing general education programs are in achieving this
generally recognized goal. In the absence of adequate empirical measures, it
has not been possible to gauge the extent to which college general education
programs achieve the intended outcomes.

The authors of this chapter assume that assessing the outcome of general education programs cannot be limited to considerations of the impact of
courses or programs of study. Successful general education programs extend
beyond the classroom, attending to both the affective and the cognitive needs
of students and encompassing services ranging from orientation activities to
remedial programs. Moreover, as the notion of general education expands to
include a whole range of student programs and services, measurement of its
impact or effectiveness becomes even more complex. A number of dimensions
relating to student achievement of general education outcomes need to be considered, including how courses are taught, what kinds of advice students

J. E. Roueche (Ed.). *A New Look at Successful Programs.* New Directions
for College Learning Assistance, no. 11. San Francisco: Jossey-Bass, March 1983.

receive about academic offerings, and what happens to students outside the classroom.

In recent years, colleges and universities have felt pressure to assure students and other constituencies that the benefits of general education outweigh the costs. To be convincing, these assurances must be based on evidence that specific general education outcomes have been achieved. The College Outcome Measures Project (COMP), developed by the American College Testing Program (ACT), provides a method for measuring the gains that students make during the general education period in the basic skills and the knowledge that has been shown to be relevant to effective functioning in adult roles after graduation. Campuses that initiate COMP assessment of student learning are excited by its potential contribution to both campus and program management.

The basic approach of COMP is to establish the relationship between standard college program features and outcome indicators. By applying key outcome indicators, such as gains in student learning as measured by COMP tests and persistence to graduation rates, COMP identifies features of successful programs to which decision makers can, with confidence, assign priority in allocating resources to general education. Further, assessment of the relative importance of these features can help faculty and administrators to design and modify such programs.

Formal assessment of learning outcomes is becoming popular. Since 1976, 160 colleges and universities have used COMP assessment instruments to conduct empirical studies, and 340 have used other COMP services. This chapter considers the process of defining and assessing outcomes of college programs and examines the findings of a study that Forrest (1982) conducted of forty-four institutions to identify features of college programs most clearly related to increased student persistence to graduation and to increased student competence to function successfully after graduation. Many of these features relate to the importance of individualized instruction and advising. Early assessment of students' basic skills and systematic placement of students in remedial programs emerge as key factors in the success of general education programs.

Design of COMP

Defining Expectations. There is much disagreement both within and across institutions among faculty, administrators, students, parents, and the public as to what to expect from general education. However, most of these participants in the general education enterprise expect at least two outcomes: first, that students should acquire the basic abilities and motivation needed to complete courses in a chosen field of concentration and other requirements for graduation or program completion successfully; second, that students should acquire the basic abilities and motivation needed to function effectively in adult roles after graduation. It would seem reasonable, then, to use measures of how well an institution is achieving these two expectations as a basis for judging the effectiveness of its general education program.

Measuring Effectiveness. Specifically, what is needed is information about the percentage of full-time entering freshmen who graduate with a bachelor's degree within five years or (at a community college) with an associate in arts degree within three years. One could argue for a longer time frame, such as ten or fifteen years. However, institutions rarely keep such data. Thus, number of degree recipients seems to be a reasonable indicator of how well an institution provides the abilities and motivation that students need to persist to graduation.

Another critical measure of effectiveness is the gains that students make over a two- to five-year period in basic skills and in knowledge shown to be relevant to effective functioning after graduation. Institutions that use COMP instruments have generally been more interested in evaluating student growth during the college enrollment period by computing a gain score on the basis of pre- and posttesting than in evaluating levels of student ability at graduation.

COMP instruments are designed to measure student learning in six general education outcome areas. In the area of communicating, they assess the student's ability to send and receive information in a variety of modes (written, graphic, oral, numeric, symbolic), a variety of settings (one-to-one, small groups, or large groups), and for a variety of purposes (to inform, to understand, to persuade, to analyze). In the area of problem solving, they assess the student's ability to analyze scientific, social, and personal problems and to select, create, and implement solutions. In the area of clarifying values, they assess the student's ability to identify personal values and the values of others, to understand how values develop, and to understand the implications of decisions based on personal values. In the area of functioning within social institutions, COMP instruments assess ability to identify institutions constituting the social aspects of culture, including governmental and economic systems, religion, and familial institutions, and to analyze one's own and others' functioning within them. In the area of using science and technology, the instruments assess the student's ability to identify activities and products constituting the scientific and technological aspects of culture, including transportation, housing, energy, and health maintenance, and to analyze personal and cultural uses of technology. Finally, in the area of using the arts, COMP instruments assess the student's ability to identify activities and products constituting the artistic aspects of culture, including graphic art, music, drama, literature, dance, and film, and to analyze the personal and cultural uses of art.

There are three COMP instruments: the Composite Examination, the Objective Test, and the Inventory Activity. Questions in the Composite Examination and the Objective Test are based on television documentaries, magazine articles, advertisements, short stories, art prints, music, discussions, and newscasts. In the Composite Examination, students respond with short written answers; long written answers (a task made more realistic to students by asking them to write letters rather than essays); oral responses, which are audiotaped; and innovative multiple-choice questions. The Objective Test consists entirely of multiple-choice questions. The Activity Inventory uses a multiple-choice self-report format to assess the quality and quantity of student participation in out-of-class activities related to the six outcome areas.

Probably the most unique feature of these COMP instruments is that they measure abilities relevant to effective functioning in adult roles. Scores correlate strongly with such indicators of effective functioning as job supervisor ratings, socioeconomic status of job, degree of participation in community volunteer activities, and amount of continuing education after graduation (Forrest and Steele, 1982).

Isolating Program Features That Contribute to Success. Because each college is unique, different factors can prove important on different campuses for achieving the twin outcomes of increasing student competence and increasing student persistence. What works at one college does not always work at another. But colleges are also similar in many ways, and so it is quite possible that some common features play significant roles in achieving program objectives, while others play secondary roles.

A Comprehensive Study

Recently, COMP completed an intensive analysis of student scores on COMP tests and persistence to graduation rates at forty-four institutions (Forrest, 1982). These institutions included liberal arts colleges at major research universities, community colleges, small private colleges, regional state universities, small selective private universities, and small public colleges. The analysis examined specific program features for their possible relationships to test score gains between entrance and graduation (increased competence) and to the percentage of freshmen who persisted to graduation (increased persistence).

Gains in average total scores between entrance and graduation ranged from zero to twenty. The typical score gain was seven. The forty-four institutions also varied considerably in the percentage of entering full-time freshmen who graduated within five years at senior colleges or within three years at community colleges, in that the percentages ranged from 40 percent to 70 percent, with the average being 52 percent.

Given this diversity in impact both on student learning and on persistence to graduation, much could be learned by examining the relationships between other general education program features and these two major outcome indicators. Of course, identifying features that distinguished highly effective programs from less effective programs would not in itself establish a

PROPERTY
COMMUNICATION SKILLS CENTER
OHIO NORTHERN UNIVERSITY.

causative link. For example, a high correlation between expenditures and score gains would not prove that spending more money would increase score gains. Identifying such relationships would, however, reveal features most likely to produce the desired effects on score gains, persistence rate, or both.

Outcome Indicators. Before we explore the relationships between specific program features and outcome indicators, it will be instructive to consider the relationships between the two key outcome indicators, score gains and rates of persistence to graduation. The study reported here verified the common assumption that they are related; that is, institutions with high score gains tend also to have high persistence to graduation rates. Institutions with above-average score gains have an average persistence to graduation rate of 58 percent, while institutions with below-average score gains have an average persistence to graduation rate of 47 percent. In much the same way, institutions with above-average persistence to graduation rates have an average score gain of 10.4, while institutions with below-average persistence to graduation rates have an average score gain of 5.9. These findings indicate that the more students learn, the more likely they are to persist to graduation. Institutions that are more productive in delivering student learning have higher persistence rates.

Program Features. The analysis of relationships between outcome variables and other program features considered three broad categories: orientation and academic advising of new students, general education curricular objectives and requirements, and instructional dimensions.

Orientation and Academic Advising of New Students. All forty-four institutions in the study identified means, including printed materials, by which they informed prospective and new students about curricular objectives and requirements of the general education program, support services, extracurricular activities, and institutional policies. These institutions differed widely, however, in the number of formal contact hours required of freshmen in orientation activities and in the degree to which freshman academic advising was administered as a distinct function. For the eight institutions that had the most comprehensive orientation and advising programs, an average of 60 percent of the full-time freshmen graduated in the three- to five-year period, while the sixteen institutions that had the least comprehensive programs had an average persistence rate of 47 percent. The most comprehensive institutions had an average score gain of 9.5, while the least comprehensive institutions had an average gain of 6.2.

While these data do not allow us to say that a more comprehensive orientation and advising program will produce greater intellectual growth and persistence among students, it does seem likely that there is a relationship. Freshmen orientation and advising do seem well suited to help students to come to an understanding of the objectives of the general education program and to make decisions about how best to benefit from the program. They also seem well suited to diagnose individual learning interests, and they provide opportunities for freshmen to establish working relationships with faculty, staff, and selected upperclassmen. A program that stresses the importance of advising to all concerned probably strengthens the commitment of both faculty and students to the general education program.

General Education Curricular Objectives and Requirements. At all forty-four institutions, catalogues and other materials for prospective students stated what students were expected to learn, regardless of their intended area of concentration. Five institutions had student-oriented goal statements, which emphasized what students needed to know in order to function effectively after graduation over specific content. These five institutions also required proficiency examinations in one or more of the general education areas. That is, they backed up the pragmatic goal statements with a quality control mechanism common to all students. At these institutions, responsibility for general education is clearly viewed as being institutionwide.

At eighteen other institutions, goal statements for general education were content-oriented. At these institutions, proficiency examinations were not required outside the context of the general education courses. The remaining twenty-one institutions in the study had student-oriented goal statements or proficiency examinations but not both.

Does the combination of student-oriented goals for general education with required proficiency examinations appear to make a difference? There was no significant difference among the three groups in rates of persistence to graduation. However, the five institutions that combined student-oriented goals with required proficiency examinations had an average score gain of 11.6, while the eighteen institutions that had neither had an average score gain of 5.9.

Again, while the study cannot state with certainty that pragmatic student-oriented goals statements backed by proficiency examinations result in greater student learning, it does seem probable that there is a relationship. It is likely that the combination of goal statements with examinations serves as an important organizer for faculty and students, giving direction to both teaching and learning efforts. The five institutions that combined goal statements with examinations are obviously intent on making clear to all concerned that general education should make a difference in students and that this clarity of purpose governs curriculum planning and evaluation.

Instructional Dimensions. Under the heading of instructional dimensions, the COMP study identified thirteen key indicators that describe the instructional programs of the forty-four institutions. Instructional dimensions include noncredit remedial courses in basic skills, student–faculty ratio, and other factors relating to how the general education curriculum is implemented. Administration and faculty can exercise considerable control over all these factors within overall budget constraints. The study found that only one instructional dimension seemed to be related to score gains and persistence rates clearly enough to have practical significance. That dimension can best be characterized as individualized instruction focused on relevant, practical skill building through the formal general education curriculum.

Individualization is indicated by two key features: First, there is systematic placement of students in remedial courses in reading, writing, and composition that provide the basic skills and knowledge needed to function effectively at the institution. These courses run a full term, not just a week or two. Some are offered for college credit; others are not. Most courses are taught by specially trained staff clearly identified with the remedial program, not by staff of a regular academic department. Second, credit-bearing off-campus general education opportunities providing generic skills and knowledge needed to function effectively in adult society are open to all students. General education requirements can also be met through field observation, internships, and on-the-job experiences. These opportunities are offered both by the traditional liberal arts departments and by more career-oriented units. Finally, student use of these options is sufficient to warrant at least a part-time institutionwide coordinator of off-campus programs.

The COMP study identified nineteen institutions that had both key features and thirteen institutions that had neither. The other twelve institutions were judged to have one key feature but not both. The institutions in each of these groups were highly diverse. However, four of the five community colleges were in the group that had both remedial courses and credit-bearing off-campus opportunities in general education.

There were no significant differences among the three groups in average entering ACT or SAT scores. The decision to offer either remedial courses or off-campus learning in general education seems not to be influenced by the academic abilities of the institution's entering freshmen. The nineteen institutions that had both remedial courses and off-campus general education opportunities had a persistence to graduation rate of 55 percent, while the thirteen institutions that had neither had a rate of 46 percent. Institutions that had both remedial courses and off-campus general education opportunities had an average score gain on the COMP tests of 8.8. Institutions that had neither had an average score gain of 4.6. Finally, there were no significant relationships between score gains or persistence rates and such voluntary and short-term academic assistance programs as tutoring or learning centers.

While the COMP study cannot affirm definite causal relationships between the thirteen instructional dimensions examined and score gains or persistence rates, it does seem likely that the most important dimension is the institution's degree of success in individualizing and focusing instruction on relevant, practical skill building within the structure of the formal general education program. Finally, it appears that students are more motivated to learn and persist to graduation if they believe that the general education program provides knowledge and skills that promise to be important to effective functioning not only at the institution but in adult roles after graduation, particularly on the job.

Recommendations

Forrest (1982) uses COMP study results to make a number of recommendations. Two of the most important will be described here. First, probably the single most important move that an institution can make to increase student persistence to graduation is to ensure that students receive the guidance that they need at the beginning of their journey through college to graduation. At its best, this guidance system includes four features: New student orientation should begin well before students arrive on campus, and it should continue as a formal course during the first term on campus. Faculty who do academic advising should be selected, trained, and compensated for that task. Orientation and academic advising should be coordinated by an administrator and a faculty committee. Finally, orientation and academic advising should, at a minimum, explore the value of general education, base course placement on tests and academic records as well as on student and institutional objectives, include career planning, and describe the services and policies of the institution.

Second, probably the single most important move that an institution can make to increase student competence and persistence simultaneously is to make an institutional commitment to individualized instruction focused on relevant skill development through the formal academic program. Such efforts can be expensive, but the payoffs to students and the institution can also be enormous. Two things deserve top priority: systematic placement of all students into general education courses, and emphasis in general education courses on structured experiences that require students to apply what they have learned. Even at elite institutions, many entering freshmen need to improve their academic survival skills — reading, writing, computing, and so forth. Students who need such skills should have special remedial courses, while advanced students should be placed in courses appropriate to their ability level. Furthermore, general education courses should provide students with ample opportunities to apply theoretical knowledge to simulations of situations that they will encounter after graduation. After the freshman year, off-campus learning experiences should be strongly encouraged, if not actually required of students.

These concrete recommendations, which point to the importance of key support systems, such as remedial programs and advising, are valuable because they derive from an exhaustive examination of features of college programs that achieve specified outcomes. This is an era of limited resources and increasing accountability. Thinking of general education in terms of achieving measurable behavioral outcomes, not as a process of getting students through a series of courses, establishes an accountability model that is likely to benefit students, the public, and the college itself.

References

Forrest, A. *Increasing Student Competence and Persistence: The Best Case For General Education.* Iowa City: American College Testing Program, 1982.

Forrest, A., and Steele, J. *Defining and Measuring General Education Knowledge and Skills.* Iowa City: American College Testing Program, 1982.

Lee Noel is executive director of the National Center for the Advancement of Educational Practices, American College Testing Program. A pioneer in research on college student retention and a nationally recognized authority in this area, he has delivered keynote addresses to more than 20,000 educators over the past five years.

Diana Saluri is a visiting assistant professor of English at the University of Iowa and an editorial assistant at the American College Testing Program.

*Practitioners and researchers suggest ways to make
developmental or basic skills programs work.*

Programs for the
Underprepared Student:
Areas of Concern

Susan Sellman Obler

In support of the commitment of community colleges to the open-door policy,
we provide programs for underprepared students. Historically, this role has
come to the community college with growing demand. Until very recently, the
senior colleges selected these students out. In contrast, the people's colleges
provided universal access and welcomed students who were limited in basic
skills and unfamiliar with academe. With apologies to Robert Frost, we
assumed the role not taken. This was part of our earliest mission, and it was
undergirded by an egalitarian philosophy that education could improve economic and social mobility. Today, this philosophy demands even more that we
respond to the needs of those who pass through the open door (Cross, 1971).
The new students bring needs as varied as their backgrounds, ages, and goals.
For many of them, schooling has been less than pleasant or productive; as a
result, some have attitudes and skills that inhibit their success. For these high-
risk students, we have begun to provide developmental and remedial programs that provide support and basic skills.

   Programs for the underprepared student have come a long way from
their pioneer days. Marginal successes have expanded into a nationwide effort
that is both more pervasive and more promising (Roueche and others, in

J. E. Roueche (Ed.). *A New Look at Successful Programs.* New Directions
for College Learning Assistance, no. 11. San Francisco: Jossey-Bass, March 1983.

press). Some critics argue that we cannot serve so many masters and that the comprehensive mission dilutes our success with individual needs. Zwerling (1976) even wonders if we are coconspirators in a plot to maintain the class-bound status quo. If he is right, we must ask why developmental and basic skills programs have had to struggle so to do the job. If we are serious about preparing students who have many skill deficiencies, this part of our mission is not likely to disappear for some time. Indeed, the Adult Performance Level Project, a national survey of adult competence, estimated that almost one fifth of America's adults are functionally incompetent (Adult Performance Level Project, 1977). The basic concerns of developmental education are closely aligned with skills described in that research: "Four primary skills seemed to account for the vast majority of requirements placed on adults. These skills were named (1) communication skills (reading, writing, speaking, and listening), (2) computation skills, (3) problem-solving skills, and (4) interpersonal relationship skills" (Adult Performance Level Project, 1977, p. 8). Developmental education, while preparing students for college work, is also teaching skills that are basic to lifelong competence. But what really works? Five major patterns seem to emerge from effective programs described in the literature: thorough assessment, systematic instruction, careful staffing, consistent evaluation, and centralized program coordination.

Thorough Assessment

Assessment seems to be fundamental and imperative. It should be as thorough as possible. Testing is still fraught with controversy. However, we have grown from civil rights paranoia to concern for congruence between mission and practice. The more we know, the better we can serve students. It can even be argued that it is immoral not to test students who might otherwise attempt advanced work, thereby committing "academic suicide" (Roueche, 1981). Moore (1976, p. 31) asserts that "a complete diagnosis is what the student has a right to expect." Increasingly, colleges are moving to mandatory assessment of all entering new students. At Sacramento City College in California, the catalogue clearly states that a full assessment of skills and aptitudes must be conducted for each student by the time the student has accumulated fifteen credits or during the first term in which the student takes more than nine credits. Fullerton College in California received a grant for a three-year study of the correlation between reading proficiency and student persistence. The final report of this study (Cordrey, 1981) concludes that testing and remediation of reading skills reduces the dropout rate in reading-dependent courses. As a result, Fullerton College has begun a program of thorough prerequisite learning skills assessment for most entering students.

Most skills assessment still occurs as screening for specific courses. Roueche and others (in press) find that more than 60 percent of the colleges surveyed nationally used preassessment in the basic skills of reading, writing, and mathematics. A study conducted by the California Postsecondary Education Commission (1982) finds mandatory assessment of writing skills in more than 59 percent of the 101 colleges surveyed. There are few coordinated, mandatory, preregistration assessment programs; rather, most existing assessment programs take a fragmented, departmental, precourse approach.

The scattered approach to locating the underprepared student allows many to slip through the net before their basic skills can be strengthened. A number of studies find that mandatory assessment and directive guidance are keys to retention. A three-year study of literacy development in community colleges (Roueche and Comstock, 1981, p. xiv) concluded that "assessment for basic skill development should not be voluntary." Cross (1971) argues that thorough, current assessment is needed because many new students have experienced such frustration and failure in past educational experiences that past records of performance, if available, are shaky measures for placement.

Which tests or measurements to use and who uses the information are not easy problems to solve. The strategies that appear to achieve the greatest success combine basic skills testing with assessment of attitudes toward learning, sometimes including self-concept. Roueche and Snow (1977, p. 88) found an "inextricable relationship of self-concept development with academic achievement." Numerous writers suggest that the typical high-risk student is failure-threatened and not likely to feel good about himself, at least as far as academic achievement is concerned. Of course, cultural bias can limit the validity of self-concept instruments. The wise practitioner will take care to avoid misunderstanding the cultural variables in self-concept appraisal (Moore, 1976). Nevertheless, there is considerable agreement among researchers that both cognitive and affective measurements are needed to create a substantial picture of the individual student's strengths and weaknesses. Without a multidimensional picture, advisement and placement cannot occur. Information is powerful, indeed. At Miami–Dade Community College, information for use in placement and academic progress is the key element in sharing responsibility with students for their success. After assessment, the college uses a very directive approach, so that "students with deficiencies are required to take necessary developmental work before proceeding to programs where lack of skill could cause failure" (McCabe, 1981, p. 10). When taken together, assessment appears to be a basic requirement for locating specific needs. It is then the role of advisement to direct students to programs and courses that can turn past limitations around and redirect goals.

Systematic Instruction

Many approaches and curricula work well in developmental and basic skills programs. Most practitioners would agree with Trillin and Associates (1980, p. 4) that "we should not rely too heavily on any one method or point of view but instead see each as a prop for performance that relies for its success not on tricks but on knowing when and how to use them." However, the most success is reported when instruction is thoroughly individualized, consistently monitored, and oriented to results. Mastery learning meets these criteria. It is especially effective with students who have been unsuccessful in past school activities. Cross (1976, p. 78) believes that "mastery learning is the critical missing link in the education of low achievers." Mastery learning has two advantages. First, a task is broken down into manageable bits that are not likely to overwhelm the uneasy learner. Second, success breeds success; each part must be mastered before the learner can advance to more difficult material. In this way, positive reinforcement compounds progress and combines cognitive and affective learning. No matter how individualized learning materials are, however, few low achievers can progress without consistent support. In their study of remedial programs, Roueche and Snow (1977) found that students' natural procrastination can affect their persistence negatively. They recommend close, caring supervision of students so that their inclination to delay work does not damage their achievement. We have to see the learner to be able to serve him; if prodding is needed, we have to deliver it.

Another important aspect of the structured curriculum is content material that is relevant to the learner's needs and goals. Such relevance is closely related to content retention. We retain what seems useful. At Linn-Benton Community College in Oregon, positive results occur when skills are connected to the specific choice of major. Johnson (1980, p. 6) reports, "Students work in the vocational skills lab until they have achieved the basic competencies necessary to survive in the regular track. This allows students to declare a major and feel they are a part of a program." This approach is supported by findings of a study at Oregon State University: "The need for materials used in the developmental program to be relevant to an individual's course of study was ranked highest of the items dealing with operational aspects" (Stetson, 1979, p. 83). Knoell and others (1976) found that 46 percent of the responding students indicated that their course work was not related to their employment or their goals. Further, most practitioners and researchers agree that interpersonal skills are often as relevant to future goals as basic skills. Cross (1976) urges that the nondirective methods associated with the 1960s be replaced with a systematic approach. As with mastery learning, sequential, highly ordered learning allows tasks to be broken down into manageable challenges.

Finally, the developmental courses must be offered for credit. Credit is the coin of our realm. The issue of whether basic skills are precollege is hotly debated. It is clear, however, that they are procollege, and for that reason they should offer the same official rewards that other courses do. Transfer credit is probably inappropriate for some basic skills courses, but elective credit is becoming more common, even in the senior colleges and universities. Roueche and others (in press) found that about 45 percent of the community colleges surveyed were awarding credit for remedial courses. High-risk students must regard these basic subjects as real college work that seriously benefits their future achievement. In fact, students' persistence in college appears to be reduced when credit is not awarded for preparatory and support courses (Roueche and Snow, 1977). Credit is symbolic of value, rigor, and respectability. It also is evidence of the institution's commitment to the underprepared student.

Careful Staffing

Three staff roles in combination appear to serve underachievers most effectively: instructional faculty, counselors, and peer tutors. Programs that are able to capitalize on the skills of all three groups are those most likely to achieve success.

Instructional faculty in developmental programs need to be involved voluntarily, and they should possess some very special qualities. In the past, as seasoned practitioners well know, the teacher in remedial programs was often the low man on the totem pole. The negative associations of remedial activities can be reinforced by those who have not chosen to teach in these programs. Roueche and Snow (1977, p. 9) put it bluntly: "It looks as if educators did everything possible to make sure that student success would be an impossibility in remedial programs." Happily, it is now rare that faculty are banished to remedial teaching. Most choose the assignment out of a sincere interest in special learning problems and high-risk students. The instructors in such programs are a special breed: succinct, specific in corrections, clear in expectations, able to listen, and unafraid to depart from traditional methods. They are accessible, visible, available — supportive and challenging at the same time (Moore, 1970). Professionals who have these qualities are open to training in the special needs of underachievers, and an institution is wise to provide it. Competence and caring are the key qualities at each staffing level.

Counselors are concerned with the affective goals of the curriculum and the reinforcement of progress. Counselors also serve developmental programs in assessment, advisement, and definition of career goals. One study (Gordon, 1975) indicates that students who had the benefits of counselors' social and psychological support demonstrated increased self-esteem and motivation while increasing their grade point averages. High-risk students often have very little idea of what to expect in the college experience, and they need "an advisor to make explicitly clear what is expected of them, what the consequences are for failure to follow certain institutional and faculty directions" (Moore, 1976, p. 37). Cross (1976) suggests that counseling staff can play a multiple role, acting as ombudsmen to other departments, as shapers of the affective curriculum, and as mentors to students. She says (Cross, 1976, p. 43), "The need for the special skills of the counseling staff cannot be overemphasized." Moore (1970) also describes the counselor as a defender of the needs of the high-risk student, an interpreter of the developmental program's goals, and a planner of staff training activities. The counselor can champion the areas of curriculum that attend to the needs of the whole person. Many underachieving students display limited self-directedness. Counselors can provide helpful activities to foster improvement in this troublesome area. For students who find it difficult to become independent learners, the transition to standard college criteria is risky at best. Counselors can protect the interpersonal, emotional aspects of learning; by doing so, they can strongly enhance academic learning.

Well-trained and carefully supervised peer tutors can fill another useful staffing role. The role of peer tutoring has expanded since the late 1960s under the influence of Carkuff (1969) and others. Carkuff sought to demythologize the role of therapist and to train nonprofessional "helpers." Many professionals, applying Carkuff's precepts to education, found that peers had an especially positive effect in the one-to-one tutoring situation. This resource remains valuable, and it is a relatively inexpensive way to get results. While modeling survival skills and successful behavior, peer tutors can also provide a range of helping skills. In fact, research at Los Angeles City College (Gold, 1980) finds that students who have peer tutors show a higher rate of achievement than students who do not. The same data also reveal strong support from faculty for the tutoring program. Similar results are reported at Los Angeles Pierce College (Schulman, 1981), where half the students indicated that they would have failed or dropped courses without peer tutoring help. The effectiveness of peer tutors is probably related to the amount of supervision and training that a program can provide to them. Programs that combine the advantages and contributions of all three staff roles—instructor, counselor, and peer tutor—seem to have the most success with underachievers.

Consistent Evaluation

Systematic evaluation of program and student progress is imperative. Effective strategies need to be made public in order to reverse the trend of noisy failures and quiet successes. Probably the most crucial element in determining what and how to evaluate is defining clear goals at the beginning. Competency-based individualized instruction allows learning activity to be divided into small components, which are easier to evaluate (Herrscher and Watkins, 1980). Program evaluation is somewhat more complicated. The question is, Which aspects of the program have accounted for what really works with individual students? Without looking at every activity in the operation, opportunities to improve systematically are limited. Gordon (1975, p. 16) agrees: "Neither the program [nor] the institution should fear the discovery of lack of quality in their practices, for without feedback it becomes impossible to improve effectiveness or justify changes in procedures and practices to reach important goals."

Unwisely, practitioners are inclined to neglect the potency of cost-effectiveness in their evaluation reports. At Westmoreland County Community College in Pennsylvania (Cicco and Associates, 1979), consultants demonstrated that the program generated more income through student retention than it cost in direct expenses. That evaluation also measured perceived benefit to the community, the program's reputation within the college, and the students' transition to mainstream courses, all with positive results.

Some researchers argue that the institution as a whole has a responsibility to expect and support thorough evaluation of developmental programs. Patterson (1980) encourages the use of many sources of data: retention and follow-up studies, student attitude measures, and comparison of achievement to prestated objectives. Dumont and others (1981) encourage practitioners to use credible measures of progress: multiple indicators, multiple-design strategies, pre- and postprogram data, short- and long-range follow-up, and appropriate comparison groups.

The researcher or practitioner who uses control groups in evaluation displays rare fortitude. Even fewer dare to include students' success rates in subsequent mainstream courses. These measures, however, will tell the tale. At North Harris County College, Houston (Reap and Covington, 1980), developmental studies students have improved their skills enough to help raise the overall completion rate in freshman-level English to 71 percent. Studies of the long-range progress of developmental students at Miami–Dade Community College (Wenzel, 1980) compare them with a control group of regular students. In spite of a third-semester drop in grade point average for the developmental students, they pass their counterparts in persistence and in credits earned by the fourth term. Whatever we measure, the current concern for quality in education and for basic skills proficiency demands that we conduct program evaluation and publish our results. The key to evaluation is rigorous follow-up, carefully designed into the total program system.

Centralized Program Coordination

The pattern of organizational control varies. Some institutions favor centralized program coordination that often places developmental courses in a separate division. The basis for central control is access to services and systematic accountability for student progress. However, most basic skills efforts take place in separate courses housed in parent departments. In the sample studied by Roueche and others (in press), only 19 percent of the community colleges had a separate academic division for basic skills. In contrast, Roueche and Snow (1977) found that more than 27 percent had a coordinated separate department. This decline can, perhaps, be attributed to the realities of declining resources, or it can indicate a shift of institutional priorities. Without a public mission statement that commits the college or district to special support for the high-risk student, developmental programs can be the first to go. Funding for separate centralized programs can be evidence of such commitment. For the students involved, a separate division can help students to negotiate the difficult transition to mainstream courses. Follow-up on students moving out of isolated remedial courses is rare and problematic (Roueche and Snow, 1977). The developmental education program at Triton College (Triton College, 1980) combines the advantages of central coordination and consistent cooperation with other academic departments. In this manner, prerequisite skills can be directly linked to courses and programs in the standard curriculum.

In contrast, a number of writers suggest that a separate department reinforces the stigma of basic skills preparation as inferior to real college work. An alternative is remediation efforts built into parent departments as an adjunct support to content areas (Friedlander, 1982). Proponents of this arrangement of basic skills services argue that it increases the likelihood with which skills are directly related to a specific course or major (Maxwell, 1979). However, while this arrangement increases the chances of relevance to career objectives for students, coordination of transition to advanced work in other departments remains a problem. Cohen (1982) suggests that this part of our mission has increased in size to the point where basic skills will be the central role for the community colleges in the next few years. As Cohen says (1982, p. 18), "It is time now to integrate developmental education into the fabric of the institution." In order to do so, Cohen recommends that all instructors integrate developmental principles into their courses and that developmental educators provide the appropriate staff training. In any case, efforts to support basic skills deficiencies will need some form of credible, central coordination in order to improve the chances of student success.

Conclusion

Clearly, the success of basic skills programs depends on many variables. Each has its champions. The literature, however, shows a surprising degree of consensus about the areas of concern for programs for underprepared students. Perhaps it is only by combining many strategies in a climate of support that such programs really will work (Trillin and Associates, 1980). Or perhaps it is special treatment itself that accounts for successes with underprepared students. Still, there are some unanswered questions. How will we maintain financial support for these programs in the face of resistance from state legislatures? How can staff development change the image and status of this part of our mission? What relationships exist between basic skills programs and the student's future, both inside and outside the academy? Should we define the point at which we can no longer defend the use of public funds for a given student? How can we present an organized front to support our efforts to provide services to these students? How can we increase success in the critical transition period between basic skills preparation and mainstream course work?

The literature asserts that something can be done for the high-risk student. New approaches are often helpful. A major shift in institutional priorities is sometimes necessary. Unless we attend to the needs of the high-risk student, the open door to community colleges will become a cruel false promise. If we can maintain quality services to all students who come through the open door, we will fulfill the promises of our earliest proponents (Cohen and Brawer, 1982). In the right climate, with the appropriate comprehensive program, this is possible.

References

Adult Performance Level Project. *Adult Performance Level Study: Final Report.* Austin: University of Texas, 1977.

American College Testing Program. *Increasing Student Competence and Persistence.* Iowa City: American College Testing Program, 1982.

California Postsecondary Education Commission. *Promises to Keep: Remedial Education in California's Public Colleges and Universities.* Sacramento: California Postsecondary Education Commission, 1982.

Carkuff, R. R. *Helping and Human Relations: A Primer for Lay and Professional Helpers.* New York: Holt, Rinehart and Winston, 1969.

Cicco and Associates. *Westmoreland County Community College Developmental Program and Evaluation.* Youngwood, Pa.: Westmoreland County Community College, 1979. (ED 186 053)

Cohen, A. M. "Ten Criticisms of Developmental Education." *ERIC Junior College Resource Review,* Spring 1982, pp. 12–19.

Cohen, A. M., and Brawer, F. B. *The American Community College.* San Francisco: Jossey-Bass, 1982.

Cordrey, L. *Final Report of the Skills Prerequisite Project.* Fullerton, Calif.: Fullerton College, 1981.

Cross, K. P. *Beyond the Open Door: New Students to Higher Education.* San Francisco: Jossey-Bass, 1971.

Cross, K. P. *Accent on Learning: Improving Instruction and Reshaping the Curriculum.* San Francisco: Jossey-Bass, 1976.

Dumont, R. G., and others. "Evaluating the Quality of Basic Skills Programs." Paper presented at the annual forum of the Association for Institutional Research, Minneapolis, May 1981. (ED 205 083)

Friedlander, J. "Coordinating Academic Support Programs with Subject Area Courses." *ERIC Junior College Resource Review,* Spring 1982, pp. 20–23.

Gold, B. K. *The LACC Tutoring Program: An Evaluation.* Research Study #80-4. Los Angeles: Los Angeles City College, 1980. (ED 186 079)

Gordon, E. W. *Opportunity Programs for the Disadvantaged in Higher Education.* Washington, D.C.: American Association for Higher Education, 1975. (ED 114 028)

Herrscher, B. R., and Watkins, K. *Competency-Based Education: An Overview.* New York: HBJ Media Systems, 1980.

Johnson, J. A. "Developmental Education: Band-Aids for the Dinosaur." In J. A. Johnson and others, *One State's Efforts to Get Serious About the High-Risk Student: Assessment, Faculty Advising, Career Planning, and Developmental Education in Oregon's Community Colleges.* Salem: Oregon State Department of Education, 1980. (ED 188 732)

Knoell, D., and others. *Through the Open Door: A Study of Patterns of Enrollment and Performance in California's Community Colleges.* Report 76-1. Sacramento: California Postsecondary Education Commission, 1976. (ED 119 752)

McCabe, R. H. "Now Is the Time to Reform the American Community College." *Community and Junior College Journal,* 1981, *51* (8), 6–10.

Maxwell, M. *Improving Student Learning Skills.* San Francisco: Jossey-Bass, 1979.

Moore, W., Jr. *Against the Odds: The High-Risk Student in the Community College.* San Francisco: Jossey-Bass, 1970

Moore, W., Jr. *Community College Response to the High-Risk Student: A Critical Reappraisal.* Washington, D.C.: American Association of Community and Junior Colleges, 1976. (ED 122 873)

Patterson, M. C. M. "A Study of Congruence Between Delphi-Validated Policies and Procedures Which Promote Learning Among High-Risk Students and Current Practices in Selected Community Colleges." Unpublished doctoral dissertation, University of Texas, Austin, 1980.

Reap, M. C., and Covington, H. C. "Evaluation of the Effectiveness of the Developmental Studies Program." Unpublished paper, North Harris County Community College, 1980. (ED 197 798)

Roueche, J. E. Address to Staff, Rio Hondo College, Whittier, Calif., March 25, 1981.

Roueche, J. E., Baker, G. A., and Roueche, S. D. *College Responses to Low-Achieving Students: A National Study.* New York: HBJ Media Systems, in press.

Roueche, J. E., and Snow, J. J. *Overcoming Learning Problems: A Guide to Developmental Education in College.* San Francisco: Jossey-Bass, 1977.

Roueche, S. D., and Comstock, V. N. *A Report on Theory and Method for the Study of Literacy Development in Community Colleges.* Technical Report NIE-400-78-0600. Austin: Program in Community College Education, University of Texas, 1981.

Schulman, S. "A Description of a Developmental Program for High-Risk Students in a Community College." Unpublished report for Pierce College, 1981. (ED 208 928)

Stetson, L. D. "An Assessment of the Attitudes and Opinions of Administrators, Content Faculty, Developmental Faculty, and Students Concerning the Developmental Education Needs of Community College Students." Unpublished doctoral dissertation, Oregon State University, 1979.

Trillin, A. S., and Associates. *Teaching Basic Skills in College: A Guide to Objectives, Skills Assessment, Course Content, Teaching Methods, Support Services, and Administration.* San Francisco: Jossey-Bass, 1980.

Triton College. *Developmental Education Program: Self Study.* River Grove, Ill.: Triton College, 1980.

Wenzel, G. G. "Evaluation of the North Campus Developmental Studies Program: Winter Term Outcomes, 1979–80." Research Report Number 10. Miami: Miami–Dade Community College, 1980.

Zwerling, S. L. *Second Best: The Crisis of the Community College.* New York: McGraw-Hill, 1976.

Susan Sellman Obler is on sabbatical leave at the University of Texas at Austin from Rio Hondo College in Whittier, California. She coordinates staff development and English placement and teaches composition.

*Low-achieving adult learners are in marked need of academic
support programs when they return to education. A sampling
of successful Texas programs reveals two sets of instructor
behavior that contribute to program success.*

Profiles of Success Among Texas Programs for Low-Achieving Students

Lynn B. Burnham

Consider a few statistics: Between 1900 and 1970, except for the years surrounding World War II, children under fifteen formed the nation's largest age
group. By 1980, the largest age group was composed of those between fifteen
and twenty-nine. By 2000, 57 percent of the population will be older than
thirty; even now, those between forty-five and sixty-four comprise 20 percent
of the population (Cross, 1979–80; Russ-Eft and Steel, 1980). Consider a few
more statistics: In 1978–79, approximately 60 million adults age twenty-five
or older attended school, and 50 percent of the men age fifty and 58 percent of
the women age fifty who were queried had recently taken a class or course
(Brocklehurst, 1979–80; Russ-Eft and Steel, 1980). It is predicted that enrollment figures for higher education will increase in the 1980s. During the decade, more than 15 million adult men and women will enter nearly 3,000
colleges and universities. A closer look at community colleges reveals that
adult part-time learners already make up most of their enrollment.

The notion of lifelong learning is implicit in one group of figures and
explicit in the other. Combining it with the fact that the average age of the
American community college student is thirty, I suggest that it is time for

J. E. Roueche (Ed.). *A New Look at Successful Programs.* New Directions
for College Learning Assistance, no. 11. San Francisco: Jossey-Bass, March 1983.

educators to become aware of the adult learner's deficiencies in order to address them effectively. The declining test scores of younger learners have been chronicled so extensively that they are now general knowledge. While we need to retain our grasp on their deficiencies, we also need to know about adult learner deficiencies. It is my view that the adult learner is best approached academically from a behavioral perspective. I will state why in this chapter.

In the past few years, discussions of illiteracy and underpreparedness have expanded to include adults whose deficiencies have been discovered as adults have returned to education. The prospect is alarming: Only 46.3 percent of adults can function in a literate society. Thus, 57 million adult Americans do not have skills adequate to perform basic tasks, almost 23 million lack competencies necessary to function in society, and 34 million can function with only limited proficiency. "When given a notice posted on a cashier's desk in a store describing the check-cashing policy for that store, more than one out of five respondents did not draw the correct conclusion from the notice" (Adult Performance Level Project, 1977, p. 21). The Adult Performance Level Project concluded (p. 43) that "approximately one of five Americans are functionally incompetent, and... about half of the adult population possesses functional competencies which are associated with at best only marginal levels of success." Detailing how illiteracy translates into restricted behavioral activity, Roueche with Mink (1980) pointed out that 23 percent of American adults between the ages of eighteen and sixty-five read at a fifth-grade level, and 32 percent read at a sixth- or seventh-grade level; only 37.6 percent can shop economically; only 48 percent understand laws and how they work; and only 48.3 percent understand the fundamentals of health care.

Skills Needed

The Adult Performance Level Project (1977) concluded that four primary skills accounted for most of the requirements placed on adults: communication skills (listening, speaking, reading, writing); computational skills; problem-solving skills; and interpersonal relationship skills. In order to achieve functional competence, an adult must master each skill area at a minimum level of application and then relate to "general knowledge areas of occupational knowledge, consumer economics, community resources, government and law, and health" (p. 9). The study concluded (p. 10) that functional competence "is directly related in a mathematical sense to success in adult life."

In a survey of senior personnel executives of major corporations, Lusterman (1977) found that executives believed that educational institutions were performing poorly what they perceived the most basic function of education to be: developing competence and skill in the use of language and the intellect. Lusterman found that more than 54 percent of the executives in the study believed that employees were deficient in language skills. Computational skills were mentioned by 24 percent, 18 percent identified nonskill aspects of work readiness as deficient, 7 percent mentioned deficiencies in interpersonal skills, and 6 percent said that employees were deficient in various intellectual and conceptual abilities. Using Bies' model of competence-based instruction, Howell and Trent (1980) studied the North Carolina community college system, and concluded essentially the same thing.

It is obvious that low-achieving adults need special support services when they return to education. Not only are many of them deficient in essential academic skills, but, as Aslanian (1980) points out, many do not know what they need to learn in order to succeed. The truth is that adults often need more support services than full-time learners "who have moved through school without interruptions and thus know the ropes and have more academic confidence" (Zwerling, 1980, p. 98). Colleges and universities that do best in the remaining years of this decade will be those that recruit vigorously and then work to retain learners through attentive counseling, considerate grading, adequate financing, and conscious teaching, which can take the form of special academic classes (Carnegie Council on Policy Studies, 1981; Noel, 1978; *Evaluative Look at Nontraditional Postsecondary Education,* 1979; Glover, 1979).

Today, the whole nation is involved in the effort to respond to learners who need to develop or refine the learning skills that are requisite for academic success. In a three-year study of English-speaking institutions of higher education in North America designed to develop a comprehensive source of information about learning centers, Sullivan (1979) found that centers or programmatic responses to underprepared learners are pervasive in American higher education. Fifty percent of the 2,878 institutions surveyed indicated that they operated at least one learning center program or unit. No one kind of institution is unique in seeking to improve student skills. Public and private two- and four-year institutions are involved in the effort. Even large four-year institutions that operate medical schools, such as the University of Missouri–Kansas City, report that as many as 70 percent of the students enrolled in certain medical courses participate in learning assistance programs or supplemental course work. Harvard, Berkeley, Stanford, and Texas are among the many universities that now provide some type of learning assistance centers (Walker, 1980).

Successful Centers

Practitioners and other experts involved in developmental education generally agree that learning centers should help to remediate the academic deficiencies of learners so that they can participate in the core curriculum and that centers should provide continuing support to learners who are taking core curriculum courses. Thus, centers represent a blend of instructional resources, instructional media, learning skills development, and tutoring and instructional development (Clowes, 1981; Matthews, 1981; Newton, 1982; Roueche and Snow, 1977; Sullivan, 1979).

Writing of learning centers in community colleges, Newton (1982,

p. 32) states that, at their best, these programs "face the reality of student populations that need additional and continuing assistance in pursuing the types of learning activities required in American higher education. In this regard... these programs represent a clearly defined break with didactic, optionless, conventional patterns of higher education instruction." It would be erroneous to infer from this that the best programs for underachievers exist in the community colleges. Yet, with their emphasis on instruction and their open-door policy, the programs of the community colleges have been more pervasive than those of other institutions. Emphasis on teaching can mean that the educative process has been examined closely and that appropriate choices about what and how to teach low-achieving learners have been made so that the end result is maximum development of individual capacity (Roueche, 1979).

The centers are charged with addressing the psychological needs as well as the academic needs of underprepared learners. The two may well be related. If they are, it is erroneous to assume that people can learn anything if they are motivated to. Even if it is not erroneous, the assumption is greatly oversimplified, as it overlooks the "failure identity" that has been cultivated by most underachievers (Maxwell, 1979; Fenton and Biggs, 1977; Snow, 1977). Maxwell (1979) pointed out that patterns for underachievers are enduring, and they do not undergo spontaneous change; only to expect people to improve is not to deal with the whole learning problem. While underachievers can appear to be opposed to learning, this is not necessarily so. They may merely be opposed to a system that has failed to meet their needs (Fenton and Biggs, 1977), and the effects may have become more apparent as the average student age has increased. Therefore, program responses that help learners to change their failure identity and that help underachievers to broaden their perspective on how learning relates to goal attainment will be perceived as most valuable. Basic conditions for promoting growth are situations in which learners are challenged and supported (Maxwell, 1979). Again, the behavioral aspect is apparent.

Two national studies conducted within a year of each other documented the success of some developmental programs in addressing needs of learners in ways that permitted them to alter their behavior and remain enrolled in institutions. The study by Roueche and Snow (1977) examined the characteristics of highly successful developmental education programs by assessing nine descriptive categories: context, philosophy, rationale, placement of learners, organizational structure, support services, curriculum, staff, and evaluation. Using information from more than 300 postsecondary institutions in the nation, the study found that five factors had a statistically significant relationship to completion of a degree or certificate program: written course objectives, which are distributed to learners; use of tutors trained in techniques that enhance the learner's positive self-concept; developmental faculty who favorably compare underachievers with other learners; explicit tactics aimed at improving the learner's self-concept; and peer counselors trained in techniques that develop positive self-concept. Six other factors were found to be related to completion of a degree or certificate program: development of a special program for developmental learners, special training programs for faculty who will work with them, making learners aware of the program's philosophy, use of part-time instructional professionals, basing tests on prestated instructional objectives, and evaluating learner success through follow-up records and assessment of attitude and self-concept development. Generalizing from the study, Roueche and Snow (1977) characterized successful programs as those that make conscious efforts to address content, instructional techniques, and teacher attitudes. Content must be perceived as useful and interesting. To this end, English, reading, and mathematics are taught "so as to reinforce students' verbal and qualitative abilities in other courses" (p. 94). Instructional techniques are individualized by teachers who are trying to help learners grow and develop as worthwhile human beings. To this end, instructors believe that underachievers can learn and accept some responsibility for increasing their desire to learn, instructors work to improve learners' self-concepts, and instructors are concerned about their own growth and development.

The second national study conducted in 1978 by the National Center for Higher Education Management, American College Testing Program (Beal, 1980), was designed to identify, compile, and analyze information about campus action programs and other efforts aimed at improving retention in higher education. The study found that improved instructional services can enhance retention. The types of programs encountered most frequently were learning skills and academic support systems (learning centers) and programs involving advising, orientation, and early warning systems. The main target groups for these programs were high-risk learners of all ages, followed by freshmen and transfer students, then by all other students. Of the fifty programs that had an improved retention rate of 10 percent or more, seventeen dealt with learning centers. Of the 420 programs with an impact index of two or more, 115 were learning and academic support programs, which had a retention index of 3.45. For programs dealing only with high-risk learners, the retention index was 3.57. The most common learning and academic support programs aimed at low-performing, high-risk learners offered a full range of services in an attempt to influence the entire behavioral repertoire: personal tutoring, credit/no credit courses, group learning sessions and laboratory sessions, learning contracts, and career-related learning services. In his generalization from data produced in the study, Beal (1980, p. 72) concluded that many programs and services discussed are already well known but that "what the reader may not realize is the potential for a direct relationship between learning centers and retention. . . . The most significant and exciting efforts appear to be directed at all students who want to improve their learning skills, whatever their level of academic performance."

Reporting from the Fund for the Improvement of Postsecondary

Education on underprepared learners, Bernstein (n.d., p. 6) observed that the most promising efforts to help the underprepared were those that worked to "integrate cognitive and affective dimensions and approach students'... needs in terms beyond success in college." Such efforts seek to establish positive behavior patterns that can be carried beyond academia. Many of these efforts concentrate on teaching learners how to learn, on enhancing self-concept, and on combining self-paced instruction with group learning.

Emphasizing Product

Operating on the assumption that one purpose of developmental education programs is to improve learners' basic skills to a point that allows them to experience academic success in the college's core curriculum, measures of program evaluation need to concentrate on assessment of product, not of process. This concentration connotes behavioral aspects. This is not to suggest that the program's process as reflected in its administrative structure is not important. Rather, concentrating on product means that, while a variety of approaches to developmental education can be totally appropriate and workable, the important measure is outcome or performance after the learner has left the program for the core curriculum. The definitive measures of a program's success, then, are gain scores and postprogram performance.

Here, developmental education must admit an irony: Many programs that practitioners experientially and intuitively recognize as good do not have the data that some believe to provide objective, quantifiable illustrations of success. The reason is obvious. Most developmental education programs grew rapidly, more in response to learner needs than to careful growth plans. As one contends with daily tasks, one often has no time or staff to go back and establish the framework that includes quantitative evaluation. Yet, often the only factor that separates the publicly recognized developmental education programs from others is the paper that provides proof, most often in the form of success data.

This statistical proof is compiled in a variety of ways. It can be just a listing without discussion. While this can be appropriate for certain purposes, I suggest that other measures of success, based on professional judgment, require a place, too. After all, inductive, qualitative, nonexperimental research that generates hypotheses is as valid in the proper setting as experimental, deductive research that tests established hypotheses (Patton, 1980).

An inductive approach was followed in a recent substudy (Burnham, in progress) of the National Study of College Responses to Low-Achieving Students at the University of Texas at Austin (Roueche and others, in press). Burnham examined transfer programs at Texas public community colleges for elements of success. Colleges selected for close examination of their developmental education programs had all indicated program commitment to helping learners acquire enough proficiency in basic skills to matriculate successfully into follow-on core curriculum courses.

There were five selection criteria. First, the programs studied used mandatory preassessment to determine appropriate placement. This preassessment speaks of the program's commitment to effecting behavioral change in learners. The requirement means that the program is unwilling to brook continued skills deficiencies and that it is willing and able to extend a helping hand to the learner's performance level, wherever that may be.

Second, the programs had attendance standards that were enforced. This enforcement indicates commitment to learner improvement through the interaction of practitioner, program, and learner. It goes beyond this, however, to suggest a commitment to developing an internal locus of control in learners, whereby they motivate themselves to behave responsibly for their learning, in part by attending class. This criterion also speaks to the active expression of concern, to caring, which signals to learners of any age that they are important and that their presence is valued.

Third, program instructors were full-time professionals. This criterion perhaps cannot be used in states that have experienced severe reductions in education budgets. Nevertheless, staffing a program with full-time professionals demonstrates administrative commitment to the program's continuity and duration and an awareness of its time and energy demands that staffing with part-timers does not concede. The demands placed on developmental educators by ongoing revisions of course materials places an unfair burden on part-time staff, because it lengthens their teaching day without returning monetary compensation to them.

Fourth, developmental courses were articulated with follow-on college courses. Establishing developmental education courses that articulate with follow-on college courses indicates the degree to which the program — perhaps the college — believes that learners are capable of expanding their experiences in academia. This articulation, an effort to avoid educational experience vacuums, also indicates the degree to which the program recognizes the value of learners' related educational experiences. Finally, this articulation indicates that the program and the college recognize that communication and math skills and the thinking patterns and processes that typify them are foundations for all learning in our culture. Articulating developmental education with core curriculum means that staff add another dimension to their activity, seeking out information about core curriculum content and requirements, designing and sequencing developmental courses so that progress from them to core curriculum is logical, and helping learners to view education as a continuum of lifelong activity, not something that starts when a book is opened and stops when the book is closed.

Fifth, program evaluation was based on the extent to which learners improved and the extent to which they were retained in the program. This double criterion suggests that the learner and program activity are mutually important partners in the learning process. Such a criterion is a tacit admission that the program is beholden to learners, that it takes its shape and parameters from their needs and its measure of effective interaction from the degree of their staying and learning.

Other criteria met by most but not all of the institutions that met the preceding five criteria were full- or part-time counseling staff in the program, an early warning system to identify potential drop-outs, full- or part-time administrators, and designation of the program as either a comprehensive department or a division.

Professional Judgments

It is not adequate merely to identify *what is* about developmental education. To do so is to resemble the quantitative quasi-experimental research that by design ignores something that developmental education professionals know to be true: The mercurial human activity and spirit with which such programs are infused sometimes defies totally objective analysis. What one can best do is to assemble as much qualitative analysis as is necessary to tell the whole human story.

In order to determine further common elements, Burnham (in progress) interviewed developmental education program directors of colleges identified by the critical selection criteria. While several categories of information were gleaned, the important one for the purposes of this chapter is program success. When queried about reasons for program success, the directors offered responses that at first seemed too simple, too obvious. On close examination, however, the tapestry of program effectiveness revealed subtle hues that formed a consistent, satisfying design. Without exception, directors identified the reason for program success with instructor behavior that was both pragmatic about program content and learners' relationship to it and warmly and personally interactive with learners. In other words, directors identified certain teacher behaviors as the single most important reason for program success. This identification parallels in a startling way the results of a study reported by Schneider and others (1981).

In the Burnham (in progress) study, one set of teacher behaviors was directed toward program content in a way that was highly pragmatic. It viewed content as a means to an end, as a way of helping learners to improve in their use of basic skills so that they could attain higher achievement levels. Instructors thus concentrated on learning outcomes, on transfer of skills. This connotes prescriptive, directive means to teach to diagnosed deficiencies, and directors indicated that staff devoted time to in-house program and curriculum design tailored to the needs of individual learners. As part of the instructors' pragmatic, prescriptive behavior in relation to program content, directors pointed to the increased and improved articulation between developmental studies and the college's core curriculum that has made instructors outside the developmental education program aware of program activity and learners' achievements. One director called this "front-line knowledge." While emphasis on transfer of skills may seem to suggest that the instructors' ultimate goal was to see that underachievers passed successfully into the core curriculum, such was not the case with these programs. The intent was even larger. Instructors emphasized program content so as to encourage those enrolled to assume responsibility for their own learning, their own success, their own behavior. Moving successfully into the core curriculum could be only one aspect of that assumed responsibility. Other aspects were that underachievers learned to view the program as a support system, that they chose to return for additional help after they had left, and that they developed realistic attitudes about competencies and performance in general. One director spoke of the positive performance and achievement expectations that instructors established for learners in these programs, citing a specific writing requirement of six paragraphs followed by more than twice as many themes, all evaluated according to prescribed and cumulative criteria that were formulated out of diagnosed needs and concerns.

One might assume that an instructor's pragmatic behavior in relation to the developmental education program requires an appropriate match between instructor and program. Directors spoke of such a match. They cited the need to be very selective in the initial hiring and placement process, the need to select only highly qualified instructors with proven experience in developmental education, the need to select instructors whose high energy level can absorb the physical and emotional demands of developmental education. Some directors cited the need for full-time instructors in order to ensure articulation with other courses and ongoing program revision. As one director put it, "We have the right people: They're committed."

The other set of instructor behaviors that directors identified as necessary for program success involved instructors' relation to developmental learners. All directors described program instructors as acting in ways that signaled interest in, respect for, and concern about learners as individuals. As one director stated, "The instructors try to be helpful, and students realize this." Directors spoke of instructors' visibility and accessibility not only during program operation but after hours as well. This can be especially important for adult learners, who often must juggle several schedules. Some instructors encouraged at-home calls if learners believed that they could not delay talking until the next class day. Directors spoke of instructors caring enough about learners to force them to stay in the program, of instructors acting in ways that made students believe that they would not allow them to quit or fail. The attitude in this behavioral instance was not a transfer of responsibility for performance from learners to instructor but rather the instructors' deliberate construction and maintenance of a personal support system that encouraged learners to behave responsibly. Directors spoke of instructors calling learners in case of absence, insisting that they be able to explain the reason for their absence coherently and logically as well as to concede that nonattendance means that skills are not learned. Instructors thus emphasized learner behavior as being both a result of and a cause of other behavior. Directors identified open communication as part of successful instructor behavior with learners, pointing out honest evaluation and information as touchstones to the relationship. Instructors first made sure that learners understood why they were in the program (one director commented that underachievers had inflated opinions of their skill level when they entered the program) and then consistently kept them informed of their progress. The technique most often identified for this transfer of information was the one-to-one conference, a means that both underscores the concern for the individual and that nurtures a relationship among adults.

To underscore behavior that expressed interest, respect, and concern, instructors were willing to give definition to learner action by allowing professional judgment to intercede when necessary. In other words, instructors were comfortable enough in their interpersonal relationships with learners that they acknowledged their distinguishing expertise when necessary, and learners were comfortable enough in their roles as adults that they acknowledged the professionalism of instructors. For example, directors spoke of teachers who personalized their behavior even more by becoming directive and using their professional judgment to determine when a learner was ready to exit the program, what courses would best enhance that learner's interests and abilities, and how the learner should address other aspects of the educational experience.

Conclusion

To isolate one or two elements as the cause of an effect is naive, uninformed, and illogical. Nevertheless, these program directors said that, in their developmental education programs and according to their own professional judgment and experience, teacher behavior was important for program success. Perhaps these programs are practicing what others are only just learning: that the adult learner responds better to certain behavioral overtures than to approaches used for so many years that they have become methodological habit. Directors of successful programs said that education needs to spend more time listening to, responding to, caring about, and helping the community college's newest and probably most permanent student, the adult learner.

References

Adult Performance Level Project. *Adult Performance Level Study: A Final Report.* Austin: University of Texas, 1977.

Aslanian, C. B., and Brickell, H. M. *Americans in Transition: Life Changes as Reasons for Adult Learning.* New York: College Entrance Examination Board, 1980.

Beal, P. E. "Learning Centers and Retention." In O. T. Lenning and R. L. Nayman (Eds.), *New Roles for Learning Assistance.* New Directions for College Learning Assistance, no. 2. San Francisco: Jossey-Bass, 1980.

Bernstein, A. *Reports from the Fund: Underprepared Students.* Washington, D.C.: Fund for the Improvement of Postsecondary Education, n.d.

Brocklehurst, N. "Reinventing the Future: Adult Educators Meet." *The College Board Review,* Winter 1979–80, *114,* 18–19.

Burnham, L. B. "The Relationship of Institutional Leadership to Selected Successful Texas Programs for Low-Achieving Students." Austin: University of Texas, in progress.

Carnegie Council on Policy Studies. *The Carnegie Council on Policy Studies in Higher Education: A Summary of Reports and Recommendations.* San Francisco: Jossey-Bass, 1981.

Clowes, D. A. "Evaluation Methodologies for Learning Assistance Programs." In C. C. Walvekar (Ed.), *Assessment of Learning Assistance Services.* New Directions for College Learning Assistance, no. 5. San Francisco: Jossey-Bass, 1981.

Cross, K. P. "Growing Gaps and Missing Links." *The College Board Review,* Winter 1979–80, *114,* 10–15.

An Evaluative Look at Nontraditional Postsecondary Education. Washington, D.C.: National Institute of Education, 1979.

Fenton, G. S., and Biggs, B. E. *Up from Underachievement.* Springfield, Ill.: Thomas, 1977.

Glover, R. *Future Needs and Goals for Adult Learning.* New York: College Entrance Examination Board, 1979.

Howell, J. D., and Trent, C. "English Competencies Needed by Vocational Students in Community Colleges and Technical Institutes." *Community College Review,* Fall 1980, *8,* 50–54.

Lusterman, S. *Education in Industry.* New York: Conference Board, 1977.

Matthews, J. M. "Becoming Professional in College-Level Learning Assistance." In F. L. Christ and M. Coda-Messerle (Eds.), *Staff Development for Learning Support Systems.* New Directions for College Learning Assistance, no. 4. San Francisco: Jossey-Bass, 1981.

Maxwell, M. *Improving Student Learning Skills: A Comprehensive Guide to Successful Practices and Programs for Increasing the Performance of Underprepared Students.* San Francisco: Jossey-Bass, 1979.

Newton, E. S. *The Case for Improved College Teaching: Instructing High-Risk College Students.* New York: Vantage Press, 1982.

Noel, L. (Ed.). *Reducing the Dropout Rate.* New Directions for Student Services, no. 3. San Francisco: Jossey-Bass, 1978.

Patton, M. Q. *Qaulitative Evaluation Methods.* Beverly Hills, Calif.: Sage, 1980.

Roueche, J. E. "What To Do About Illiteracy." *Teaching Times,* Fall 1979, *2,* 3–9.

Roueche, J. E., Baker, G. A., and Roueche, S. D. *National Study of College Responses to Low-Achieving Students.* New York: Harcourt, Brace, Jovanovich, in press.

Roueche, J. E., and Snow, J. J. *Overcoming Learning Problems: A Guide to Developmental Education in College.* San Francisco: Jossey-Bass, 1977.

Roueche, J. E., with Mink, O. G. *Holistic Literacy in College Teaching.* New York: Media Systems, 1980.

Russ-Eft, D. F., and Steel, L. M. "Contribution of Education to Adults' Quality of Life." *Educational Gerontology,* 1980, *5,* 189–209.

Schneider, C., Klemp, G. O., Jr., and Kastendiek, S. *The Balancing Act: Competencies of Effective Teachers and Mentors in Degree Programs for Adults.* Chicago: Center for Continuing Education, University of Chicago, and Boston: McBer, 1981.

Snow, J. J. "Counseling the High-Risk Student." In J. E. Roueche (Ed.) *Increasing Basic Skills by Developmental Studies.* New Directions for Higher Education, no. 20. San Francisco: Jossey-Bass, 1977.

Sullivan, L. L. *Sullivan's Guide to Learning Centers in Higher Education.* Portsmouth, N.H.: Entelek Wark-Whidden House, 1979.

Walker, C. "The Learning Assistance Center in a Selective Institution." In K. V. Lauridsen (Ed.), *Examining the Scope of Learning Centers.* New Directions for College Learning Assistance, no. 1. San Francisco: Jossey-Bass, 1980.

Zwerling, L. S. "The New 'New Student': The Working Adult." In G. B. Vaughan (Ed.), *Questioning the Community College Role.* New Directions for Community Colleges, no. 32. San Francisco: Jossey-Bass, 1980.

Lynn B. Burnham is a codirector with National Institute for Staff and Organizational Development (NISOD) and editor of Linkages *at the University of Texas, Austin. She has been a curriculum developer, director, instructor, and evaluator in higher education.*

Developmental education programs must be as comprehensive in design as their students are diverse if either are to succeed.

Student Success at Triton College

Phoebe Knight Helm
Sunil Chand

Triton College is a community college located in River Grove, Illinois. It serves a population of approximately 300,000 citizens in the western suburbs of Cook County, adjacent to the Chicago metropolitan area. Its 26,000 students are enrolled in one of three major areas: the School of Arts and Sciences/ University Transfer Studies, the School of Career Education, or the School of Continuing Education (noncredit). Approximately 10 percent of the credit-seeking students are enrolled in the developmental education program, which is located in the School of Arts and Sciences. The needs of non–credit seeking students enrolled in continuing education will not be addressed in this chapter.

Developmental Education at Triton

The developmental education program at Triton College fits Boylan's holistic definition (1981, p. 5) in that it provides not only basic skills courses but learning assistance activities, such as tutoring and counseling and academic advising as well. Students enrolled in the program are typically described as high-risk (Roueche and Snow, 1977) in that they lack the basic skills necessary to negotiate college course work successfully. (The section on assessment and placement later in this chapter describes how students are selected for program participation.) These students include nonnative English speakers, learning disabled students, and physically disabled students.

J. E. Roueche (Ed.). *A New Look at Successful Programs.* New Directions for College Learning Assistance, no. 11. San Francisco: Jossey-Bass, March 1983.

The program is staffed with full- and part-time faculty from the English and mathematics departments, who are assigned to teach program courses, and an assistant director, who reports to the associate dean of arts and sciences. The learning assistance center houses all additional support personnel, including a supervisor, instructional assistants, tutors, proctors, special needs personnel, a counselor, and an adviser. Both the classrooms and the learning assistance center are located on the second floor of one of the main classroom buildings, adjacent to faculty offices and in the central flow of all credit students and college faculty. The program is funded by federal, state, and local dollars, with the respective shares being 20 percent, 40 percent, and 40 percent.

Program Components

The program is designed to be comprehensive. The paragraphs that follow describe individual components, both to clarify this study and to permit the program to be compared with other programs.

Assessment/Placement. Mandatory student assessment and placement occurs at two levels: in preregistration for all credit-seeking students and through pre and post in-class assessments administered in all basic skills classes. Assessment during preregistration is used to place students in courses that encourage success. All credit-seeking students take the Reading Progress Scale (Carver, 1975) and an in-house Mathematics Department Placement Test (Triton College, 1976). For the few students who have recent ACT scores, the social science and English subscores can be used. Students who score below four on the Reading Progress Scale or below sixteen on the ACT subtests and students who score below seven on the mathematics placement test are placed in the appropriate reading, writing, and mathematics courses in the developmental program. Students who score above these cutoff points enroll in the credit courses of their choice.

In-class assessment is conducted during the first week of class in all developmental, mathematics, and rhetoric classes to determine accuracy of placement and instructional needs and again at the end of the semester to determine competencies met and to estimate information gained. The Nelson-Denny Reading Test (Nelson and others, 1973) is used in the reading classes, a three- to five-paragraph essay with a uniform grading scale is used in the writing classes, and a mathematics test is used in the mathematics classes. Investigations of the accuracy of initial assessment and placement of students indicate between 90 and 96 percent agreement with faculty judgment and the in-class pretest assessment. The approximately 4 percent to 10 percent of students who are misplaced are moved to appropriate courses during the first ten days of the semester.

Counseling and Advising. A counselor and an adviser are located in the learning assistance center. The counselor assists students with career, personal, and financial decisions and teaches classes in personal and career development. The adviser assists students with academic planning and scheduling. Locating the counselor and adviser in the learning assistance center emphasizes their role as the hub of student life. It facilitates frequent interactions with faculty, students, and tutors, and it thereby promotes a team approach to student success. Maintenance of reporting lines to the assistant dean of counseling and the associate director of admissions supports a necessary information flow and provides liaisons with the entire college, maintaining the developmental program as a visible and viable component of the students' academic experience.

Developmental Courses. Six developmental courses — two in reading, two in mathematics, and two in writing — carry three semester hours of internal credit each. This credit counts toward the students' load and grade point average but not toward graduation. Exit requirements for these courses are as follows: a reading score of eleven on the Nelson-Denny Reading Test; 80 percent or better on the mathematics test, with at least one half of all word problems completed correctly; and a three- to five-paragraph essay with all the holistic components of writing evident and with a minimum number of mechanical errors. Most students complete these requirements in one semester. Others need two or more semesters, while a few students complete the requirements in less than one semester.

Tutorial Services. Tutorial services are provided by the learning assistance center in three modes — in-class, small group, and individually — for all students enrolled in credit courses at the college. Students in program courses are encouraged to use these services.

Staff Development. The developmental program provides training and development opportunities for faculty through on-campus workshops, subscriptions to professional journals, and support for attendance at local, state, and national conferences. All faculty and staff are evaluated periodically by their students and supervisors. Following the evaluation, an individual developmental or growth plan is developed with the assistance of the supervisor.

Program Evaluation

The first two years of the developmental education program were evaluated in the 1980–81 school year with the Triton College program review system (Lemoine, 1979). This system included three primary components: self-study; external review by professionals in developmental education outside the college; and a collegewide review committee of college professionals who were not members of the developmental program staff, summary of whose findings was submitted to the vice-president of academic affairs. All data reported here were taken from the 1980–81 study (Chand and Helm, 1981).

Subjects. The 1,273 students included in the study were first-time enrollees in the developmental program in fall 1978, and they were taking at least one developmental course.

Definitions. Retention is considered under two categories, completion and persistence. Completion is defined as completion of one or more developmental courses with a grade of A, B, C, D, or P. Persistence is defined as returning to Triton and earning credit in subsequent semesters. The designation of the student as successful or unsuccessful was based on the student's performance in the fall 1978 semester. Successful students earned a grade of A, B, C, D, or P in one or more developmental courses, while unsuccessful students earned a trade of I, F, R, or W in all developmental courses in which they were enrolled. For purposes of the follow-up study, students were retained in their designated category throughout the two-year period, even if they succeeded in a developmental course during a subsequent semester. Findings are reported for successful and unsuccessful students as just defined.

Findings. Completion and persistence rates for the four semesters included in the study are as follows: Of the 1,273 students enrolled, 957 (75.2 percent) successfully completed one or more developmental courses in the fall 1978 semester. The remaining 316 (24.8 percent) were not successful in their attempt to complete a developmental course during that semester.

Among students in the successful group, 846 (92.6 percent) persisted for at least one more semester, while 177 students in the unsuccessful group (56.6 percent) persisted for at least one more semester. Thus, of the initial 1,273 students enrolled, 1,023 (80 percent) earned credit in at least one more semester at Triton. Again, among students in the successful group, 719 (75.1 percent) earned credit in at least two additional semesters, as did 212 (38.9 percent) of the unsuccessful students. Thus, 846 of the initial 1,273 enrolled (66 percent) persisted for two additional semesters at Triton. Finally, among students in the successful group, 586 (61.2 percent) persisted for three additional semesters, as compared with 72 (22.8 percent) of the unsuccessful students. Thus, of the initial 1,273 students enrolled, 658 (52 percent) earned credit in three additional semesters at Triton. Since the study covered the period between fall 1978 and spring 1980, these students were enrolled and earned credit in four consecutive semesters at Triton.

Comparisons. While no direct comparisons can be made between student completion or persistence rates at Triton as a whole and developmental or community colleges across the nation due to inconsistencies among definitions and data collected and reported, some general comparisons can.

The persistence rate of credit students at Triton, including developmental students but excluding noncredit continuing education students, between fall and spring averages 69 percent. The persistence rate for developmental students at Triton, as defined by fall tenth-day enrollment and spring final grade reports — this group includes only students who returned and earned credit in spring — ranged between 84 and 89 percent over all four years of the program's existence.

National studies of attrition (Astin, 1975; Beal and Noel, 1980; Roueche and Snow, 1977) indicate that community colleges lose between

40 and 50 percent of their entering students between the fall and spring semesters and that this number increases to as much as 70 percent between the spring semester of the first year and the fall semester of the second year. While the authors would in no way wish to accept credit for all the factors that contribute to a student's decision to stay in school or leave (Boylan, 1981, p. 10), the data reported in this study seem to support Astin's (1975, p. 148) statement that "anything that can be done to enhance students' academic performance will also tend to reduce attrition rates."

Conclusion

Clearly, the purpose of program evaluation is to aid in decision making, as Moore (1981, p. 42) has discussed. The primary focus of the evaluation described in this chapter was to determine whether the goal of improving completion and persistence rates of high-risk students had been attained. However, in addition to this product type of evaluation, the evaluation process addressed other matters as well. These matters included program cost-effectiveness, staffing levels, reporting lines, clarity of job descriptions, quality of program components, and the program's ability to meet the needs of certain types of students.

It was determined that the unit cost per credit hour was approximately $26 and that the cost per tutorial contact hour was approximately $1.80. The total program revenue exceeded its expenditures. Even without considering the increased revenue generated through increased retention of students, it was evident that the program was both cost-effective and much less expensive than many technical and career programs.

As a result of the evaluation findings, staff were added, job descriptions were revised and upgraded, and reporting lines were clarified. The relatively low completion rate in the mathematics courses, which had the highest enrollment but the lowest completion rate—between 40 and 50 percent—led both the mathematics courses and the manner in which they were scheduled to be revised, and development activities for mathematics faculty and staff were added. Current data indicate an increase of approximately 24 percent in the completion rate for these courses. In addition, program personnel began to identify certain students as the highest of the high-risk; these were students whom faculty identified at the end of the fourth or fifth week of the semester as not likely to complete the semester successfully. These students (approximately 20 percent of the total enrollment) were targeted for special services from a team consisting of the counselor, the adviser, tutors, and instructors. Current data indicate that approximately 60 percent of these students complete their courses successfully.

For all these reasons, it seems valid to conclude not only that the program works but that program evaluation, when it is approached with an open mind and tough questions, can result in a program that works even better.

48

References

Astin, A. W. *Preventing Students from Dropping Out.* San Francisco: Jossey-Bass, 1975.

Beal, P. E., and Noel, L. *What Works in Student Retention.* American College Testing Program and National Center for Higher Education Management Systems, 1980.

Boylan, H. A. "Program Evaluation: Issues, Needs, and Realities." In C. C. Walvekar (Ed.), *Assessment of Learning Assistance Services.* New Directions for College Learning Assistance, no. 5. San Francisco: Jossey-Bass, 1981.

Carver, R. P. *The Reading Progress Scale.* Kansas City, Mo.: Revrac, 1975.

Chand, S., and Helm, P. K. *Developmental Education Program: Self-Study.* River Grove, Ill.: Triton College, 1981.

Lemoine, M. *Program Review.* River Grove, Ill.: Triton College, 1979.

Moore, R. L. "Role and Scope of Evaluation." In C. C. Walvekar (Ed.), *Assessment of Learning Assistance Services.* New Directions for College Learning Assistance, no. 5. San Francisco: Jossey-Bass, 1981.

Nelson, M. J., Denny, E. C., and Brown, J. I. *Nelson-Denny Reading Test.* Boston: Houghton Mifflin, 1973.

Roueche, J. E., and Snow, J. J. *Overcoming Learning Problems: A Guide to Developmental Education in College.* San Francisco: Jossey-Bass, 1977.

Triton College. *Mathematics Placement Test.* River Grove, Ill.: Triton College, 1976.

Phoebe Knight Helm is associate dean of the School of Arts and Sciences, Triton College. She designed and implemented its developmental education program.

Sunil Chand is assistant director of the Triton College developmental education program.

A combination of program strategies proves effective
at the University of Wisconsin–Parkside.

The University of
Wisconsin–Parkside
College Skills Program

Carol J. Cashen

The Wisconsin idea embodies the philosophy that the boundaries of the campus are the boundaries of the state. This idea is the foundation for the University of Wisconsin system, which consists of thirteen degree-granting campuses and thirteen two-year centers. The University of Wisconsin–Parkside (UW–Parkside) broadened the idea that education should by physically available throughout the state to the idea that education should be available to all who have the motivation to learn and the ability to succeed. Education should not be denied to prospective students who are underprepared at the time of admission. The UW–Parkside idea is called the *college skills program*. This chapter describes the development and initial evaluation of that program.

Demographics

The University of Wisconsin–Parkside opened in 1968. It is located in southeastern Wisconsin along the urban corridor that stretches from Milwaukee to Chicago. It serves commuter students from Racine and Kenosha. These cities, each with a population of approximately 90,000, are comprised primarily of small businesses and industries. To serve this industrial urban

J. E. Roueche (Ed.). *A New Look at Successful Programs.* New Directions
for College Learning Assistance, no. 11. San Francisco: Jossey-Bass, March 1983.

society, UW–Parkside emphasizes study in business, engineering technology, and science. The majority of the students, who come from five feeder high schools, are first-generation college students.

University enrollment ranges between 5,000 and 6,000 students, most of whom work, many full-time while attending school. Nearly 40 percent of the students are over age twenty-five. Because of work and family responsibilities, about 50 percent of the students take less than a full-time course load, which can extend their undergraduate education to six years or more.

The Program

Program Rationale. In the mid seventies, a primary concern of faculty was the lack of basic skills that students brought to their university studies. This lack of skills, which was not endemic to UW–Parkside, has been described as the equal opportunity disadvantage. It resulted from a variety of factors, including an influx of veterans following several wars; the establishment of open admissions policies; high school curriculum changes, especially in English; and changes in high school graduation requirements. Thus, by 1975, UW–Parkside faculty were claiming that students in upper division courses could not read, write, or perform mathematical computations at the level necessary to read college textbooks, write essays or term papers, or understand, much less perform, statistical analysis.

Several options for correcting the skills decline were explored: Higher admissions standards could be instituted, but that would close the educational door to many in the community. Appropriate level course requirements could be maintained, but that would cause those who lacked basic skills to fail. Junior and senior course standards could be lowered, but that would result in watered-down courses requiring little reading, no writing, and no mathematical computation, and the end product would be a meaningless baccalaureate degree. None of these solutions was acceptable. Instead, a fourth option was promulgated, the Collegiate Skills Program.

The rationale for the program is that students who are capable of earning a degree should not be denied access to a college education. By implication, students who are admitted to the university are capable of earning a baccalaureate degree. However, since UW–Parkside maintains an open admissions policy, students enter with a wide variety of skills levels. Yet, a student requires certain levels of skills in order to succeed in upper division course work, no matter what the student's declared major. Thus, students who lack the specific skills levels should be provided with an opportunity to attain them before beginning junior-level courses.

Program Description. The UW–Parkside program requires all matriculant students to demonstrate competence in the skills of reading, writing, mathematics, bibliographical study, and research by the time they earn forty-five credits.

To demonstrate competence, they pass tests in the first four skills and write an acceptable research paper. The skills tests measure students' ability to read and comprehend college-level material and to use appropriate skills to derive meaning from form and content. They measure students' ability to meet appropriate standards of usage in writing; to write in a manner that is clear, fluent, and exact; to compose an essay that is appropriate to its subject, purpose, audience; that contains a thesis or controlling idea; that confines its material to the subject; and that is well organized and fully developed; and to employ the narrative, expository, and argumentative forms and the kind and level of subject matter that are called for in college-level writing. They measure students' proficiency both in simple algebraic manipulations and in the analysis and solution of quantitative problems. Finally, they measure students' ability to use the appropriate resources and services of the university library to identify, select, and locate materials, both print and nonprint, on a variety of subjects and to write a college-level library research paper.

Three levels of competence have been defined for each of the five skills areas. Level I competence is the level normally expected of entering students. Students who do not meet this level in reading, usage, and mathematics as measured by placement tests are required to begin remedial work within their first fifteen credits. Students who fall below this level in other areas must begin remediation within their first thirty credits. Level II competence is the minimal level of competence in all five skills areas required for success in advanced courses. Students who fail to demonstrate this level of competence by the time they have acquired forty-five credits are placed in collegiate skills probation. If they have not remedied the deficiency by the time they have sixty credits, they are dropped for one semester. Level III competence, created to allow disciplines the authority to designate particular higher levels of competence in a given area for their majors, is still in the developmental phase.

Program Implementation. The Collegiate Skills Program was implemented in fall 1977. All matriculant students who entered at that date were subject to its requirements. Placement tests are required prior to course advising and registration. The Wisconsin English Placement Test designed by UW English faculty, the Mathematics Placement Test designed by UW–Parkside mathematics faculty, and the Nelson-Denny Reading Test are used in testing. These tests determine the most appropriate beginning-level course in a sequence of mathematics and English courses that prepare students for the competence requirements. The sequences include both remedial courses and courses that develop level II skills necessary for upper division course work. Thus, students can enter either at the basic skills level or at the more advanced level. Graduation credit is not given for remedial courses. Students who test out of level II skills are advised to take the competence tests during their first semester on campus. The flow from placement tests through English and mathematics course sequences to competence tests is shown in Figures 1 and 2.

Competence Tests. The mathematics and library skills competence tests

Figure 1. Competence Test Flow Chart: English

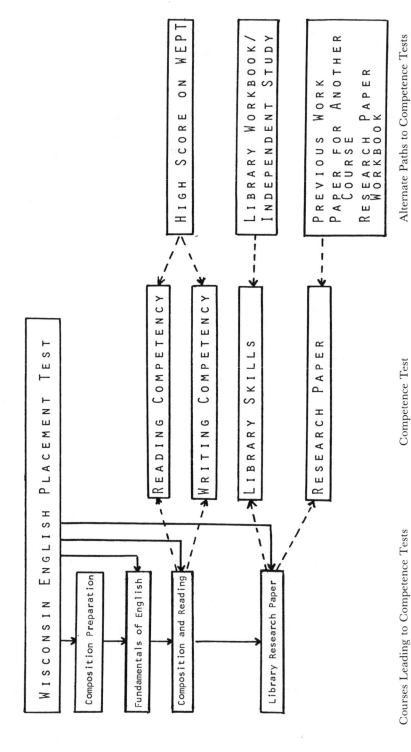

Wisconsin English Placement Test

Composition Preparation

Fundamentals of English

Composition and Reading

Library Research Paper

Reading Competency

Writing Competency

Library Skills

Research Paper

High Score on WEPT

Library Workbook / Independent Study

Previous Work Paper for Another Course
Research Paper Workbook

Courses Leading to Competence Tests

Competence Test

Alternate Paths to Competence Tests

Figure 2. Competence Test Flow Chart: Mathematics

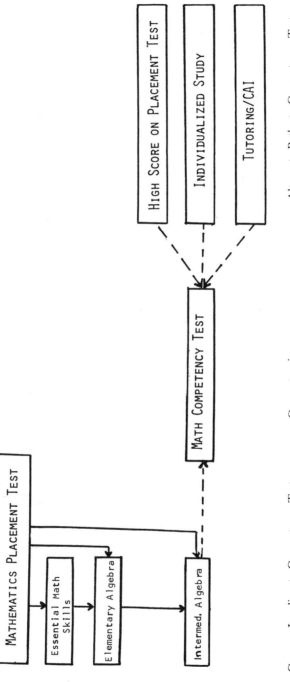

Mathematics Placement Test

Essential Math Skills

Elementary Algebra

Intermed. Algebra

Math Competency Test

High Score on Placement Test

Individualized Study

Tutoring/CAI

Courses Leading to Competence Test   Competencies   Alternate Paths to Competence Test are objective; a series of parallel forms alternates each testing period. The reading and the writing competence tests are subjective, and the results are read by pairs of readers from the English faculty. Any test on which readers disagree is assigned to a third reader, usually the student's instructor. For both the reading and the writing competence tests, the questions remain the same for each testing period, but the essay to be read for the reading test and the topic to be discussed in the writing test change with each test.

The research paper competence test can be passed by completing successfully the Library Research Paper course, in which the library skills test is given and a research paper is written; by writing a research paper in the context of another course; or by submitting a paper written previously. If a student elects not to take the research course, the student must prove competence in library skills by passing that test in addition to writing the research paper.

Students can pass any of the collegiate skills requirements without taking preparatory courses, provided that placement tests indicate appropriate preparation. Students who fail competence tests are not allowed to retake them until they have reviewed the reasons for failure and remedied their deficiencies.

Program Evaluation

Because of the unique nature of the UW–Parkside student body and the brief period that the program has been in effect, a summative evaluation of the collegiate skills program is not appropriate. With enrollment split almost equally between full-time and part-time students and with more than 40 percent of the student body taking more than four years to complete undergraduate education, a few more years will be required before summative evaluation should be undertaken. Therefore, the initial program evaluation was formative, and it followed a naturalistic design described by Wolfe (1979).

The evaluation focused on the question, What difference has the collegiate skills program made? Specifically, the evaluation sought to determine its impact on UW–Parkside faculty, academic standards, curriculum, and students. It also evaluated the program's impact on the English and mathematics curriculum of major feeder high schools in Racine and Kenosha.

Impact on UW–Parkside Faculty. Faculty were surveyed regarding their attitude toward the collegiate skills program four years after its inception. The results show that faculty are overwhelmingly in favor of the program, with 85 percent of the respondents stating that they approve or strongly approve of it. This finding parallels faculty support for the program at the time of its inception.

Impact on Academic Standards. The next question investigated was whether UW–Parkside students today are better prepared in English, library skills, and mathematics under collegiate skills than they were before the program began. Faculty who were questioned stated that students are comparably or better prepared in English and library skills today than they were under past requirements. However, students are only comparably prepared in mathematics. The reason for this disparity has yet to be determined. It has been suggested that mathematics is a very exact science and that measurement of mathematics skills is more objective than measurement of reading and writing skills.

Impact on Curriculum. After five years of implementation, the collegiate skills program is affecting the curriculum positively. The impact is most noticeable in upper division course prerequisites, in that many now incorporate a variety of collegiate skills requirements. For example, to register for an art history course in which a research paper is required, a student must have passed the competence requirements in writing and research. Faculty who teach the course are thus assured that students have the necessary tools to conduct appropriate research and to write the paper.

Impact on UW–Parkside Students. A sample of survey responses from junior and senior students indicates that they are positive about the collegiate skills program in general and very positive about the English and mathematics courses designed to develop their skills in reading, writing, mathematics, and library research. Many junior and senior students also suggest that the program reinforces their view that UW–Parkside cares about the quality of education. Some students indicated that they had originally planned to transfer to other schools but that they decided to complete their education at UW–Parkside because of the collegiate skills program.

Impact on English and Mathematics Curriculum at Area High Schools. Counselors, English teachers, and mathematics teachers generally agree that more students are taking college preparatory courses today than they were before 1977. Equally important, 90 percent of the English teachers questioned stated that there have been significant changes in the English curriculum since 1977, due in part to school district pressures for reform and in part to national concern for the skills decline, which was the major impetus for the development of the UW–Parkside program. At least half of the English elective courses have been eliminated, with the result that students have fewer, more demanding courses with which to satisfy their English graduation requirements. Most important, in both eleventh and twelfth grades, students are required to take one semester of English emphasizing composition and one semester of English emphasizing reading. The mathematics instructors interviewed stated that no major curriculum changes had occurred since 1977; however, more students today are taking mathematics beyond tenth-grade geometry.

Statistical Data. In addition to the naturalistic data collected through surveys and interviews, statistics relating to enrollment, placement, and student persistence were collected to assist in program evaluation.

Enrollment and Placement. Enrollment at UW–Parkside has not declined as a result of program implementation, as some had predicted that it would. Indeed, for the past two years, enrollment has increased beyond state projections.

Placement scores appear to be improving, especially in English, which may reflect the more rigid high school English requirements imposed at feeder high schools. While the number of students who place into remedial English has remained fairly constant — approximately 10 percent of those tested — more students are testing into the course Reading and Composition, which is regarded as freshman English; the percentage rose from 46 percent in 1980 to 49 percent in 1981. That percentage held constant in 1982.

In mathematics, approximately 10 percent of the students place into the basic remedial mathematics course, with 50 percent placing into either elementary or intermediate algebra. More important, enrollment in intermediate algebra has increased 40 percent since 1977, indicating that entering students are better prepared. The 40 percent increase in UW–Parkside students who enroll in college algebra since 1977 is also important, since the total enrollment at UW–Parkside has remained fairly constant.

Student Persistence. The success of a skills development program is usually measured by maintenance of a satisfactory grade point average and by persistence to completion of a degree. At UW–Parkside, success is also measured by the passing of competence tests. As part of the preliminary program evaluation, a pilot study of two groups of students enrolled in 1978 and 1979 was conducted in fall 1982. One group was measured for success in English, and the other group was measured for success in mathematics.

The group measured for success in English consisted of students who received grades in the Composition Preparation course in 1978 and 1979. The success criterion was defined as passing the competence tests in reading and writing, which are included in the English curriculum as part of the freshman English course entitled Reading and Composition. Data showed that 12 percent of the students in this group had passed all five competence tests, 18 percent had passed both the reading and the writing competence tests, and 28 percent had passed either the reading competence test or the writing competence test. Sixty-one percent had not attempted either test, which suggests that these students had not yet enrolled in Reading and Composition.

The group measured for success in mathematics was a random sample of students receiving grades in fall 1978 in the sequence of courses leading to the mathematics competence test. Again, success was defined as passing the competence test in mathematics. Data showed that 52 percent of the students passed the mathematics competence test. Eleven percent failed it, and 37 percent had not attempted it.

Analysis. The fairly high percentage of students who had not attempted the competence tests reflects a significant trend at UW–Parkside, the stopout trend. Students stop taking courses for one or more semesters due to family concerns, work schedules, or financial pressures and then return later to continue their studies. As a result of this trend, many enrolled students, particularly those who place in remedial classes, do not move through their baccalaureate education in the traditional four-year period. Data from 1982 show that, three to four years after taking Composition Preparation, 56 percent of these students had earned fewer than twenty-five cumulative credit hours. However, 53 percent had a grade point average of 2.01 or better, and two-thirds had completed courses within the last year and a half. Thus, although these students do not move through UW–Parkside quickly, they are maintaining satisfactory grade point averages, and they are persisting.

The most cogent claim for maintaining the remedial phase of the collegiate skills program is the fact that, of the 28 percent of the students who passed both the reading and the writing competence tests, 47 percent ranked lower than the fiftieth percentile in their high school class, with 24 percent ranking in the bottom quartile. Many colleges and universities will not admit students in the bottom quartile, yet this study suggests that, given adequate skills training, they can succeed in college. Of the 47 percent who ranked lower than the fiftieth percentile, 63 percent passed all five competence tests, thus demonstrating their ability to complete studies for a baccalaureate degree.

Projection. A projection based on analysis of cumulative grade point average, credit hours earned, and persistence suggests that an additional 23 percent of the students analyzed for success in English and in mathematics had a sufficient grade point average and persistence to warrant the assumption that they will pass the respective competence tests. If this projection is accurate, the success rate for English will increase to 51 percent and the success rate for mathematics will increase to 75 percent. A success rate of 50 percent for a high-risk student group is more than satisfactory, while 75 percent in phenomenal.

Summary

Data from a comprehensive formative evaluation and a pilot statistical study suggest that the Collegiate Skills Program is successful. The positive aspects of the program are reflected by overwhelming faculty support and by the belief that students are performing comparably or better under the Collegiate Skills Program than under previous requirements; by students' success rate and by students' strong support for the program; and by the curriculum changes implemented in English at feeder high schools.

In the five years that the program has been in effect, it has moved from a concept to a reality. All students, but especially underprepared students and returning nontraditional students, gain confidence in their ability to complete the baccalaureate degree by passing the competence tests. Faculty who teach upper division courses are assured of students' competence in the areas of reading, writing, mathematics, bibliographical study, and research.

Reference

Wolfe, R. Unpublished report on Strategies for Conducting Naturalistic Evaluation in Socio-Educational Settings: The Naturalistic Interview prepared by invitation for publication in the Occasional Paper Series, Evaluation Center, Western Michigan University. Indiana University, May 1979.

Carol J. Cashen is director of educational program support at the University of Wisconsin–Parkside.

*With decreasing college enrollment a certainty in the current decade,
institutions must look for ways of reducing student attrition.
Intrusive advising has been an effective solution on many campuses.*

Effective Outcome Measures of Intrusive Advising Programs

Robert E. Glennen

College enrollments will decline nationally by about 15 percent between now
and the mid 1990s (Breneman, 1982). All elements of higher education are
familiar with the demographic character of the coming decade. It is predicted
that the eighteen- to twenty-one-year-old customary student population will
shrink by 25 percent, and it is unlikely that the number of students who
actually finish high school will increase. In fact, the number of students who
finish high school is decreasing. It is also unlikely that the proportion of those
who finish high school and want to go to college will rise in the coming decade
to offset the loss in absolute numbers.

Very few colleges experienced enrollment decreases until the early seventies. The baby boom generation has matriculated through college, and for
the next decade most institutions face declining enrollments. Most colleges are
unwilling to believe that their own enrollment will decrease, although they do
expect that other universities will have trouble during the current decade.
However, if universities operate under the assumption that declining enrollment is someone else's problem, they are in for a big surprise. The enrollment
decrease has severe budget implications for schools, because most states operate on a formula budgeting system. Therefore, the fewer students that an
institution has, the less money it is going to receive from the legislature. For
private schools, declining enrollment means declining tuition revenues.

J. E. Roueche (Ed.). *A New Look at Successful Programs.* New Directions
for College Learning Assistance, no. 11. San Francisco: Jossey-Bass, March 1983.

These demographics are discouraging news for colleges and universities. However, college admission offices cannot be faulted. They are not responsible for the unfavorable demographics, and we cannot expect them to bear the burden of being excessively market wise and expanding their recruiting efforts. Generally, they have performed admirably. Their results include a remarkable expansion of access to higher education for women, racial and ethnic minorities, low-income students, and older part-time students. Approximately 25 percent of those enrolled on college campuses today are people over twenty-five years of age, a positive trend that is predicted to continue.

The factors that colleges have to consider when making enrollment projections are high school graduation rates, college entry rates, college retention rates, enrollment rates for older students, enrollment of foreign students, enrollment of graduate students, and full-time enrollment as compared to part-time enrollment. Other factors that influence enrollment increases under current economic conditions are the heavy impact of inflation, the rising cost of college attendance, changes in financial aid, and the ongoing concern among young people about the value of a college education (Breneman, 1982). Other demographic factors that affect enrollment patterns are the state of the economy and the rate of increase in the cost of college attendance relative to the general inflation rate and the growth of family income. The quality and diversity of academic programs as well as the location and prestige of the institution also have an effect.

Student Retention

The most promising strategy for boosting university enrollment is to increase the retention rate of students already enrolled. It is obvious that students who leave a university are capable academically, or they would not have been admitted in the first place. Therefore, institutions need to look at how to retain such students. While the attrition problem can never be eliminated completely, most colleges can do a better job of retaining their currently enrolled students, since this is one area in which colleges can exercise considerable control. The Carnegie Council (1980) indicated that six out of ten students who enroll in college fail to get their degrees. Summerskill (1962) reviewed thirty-five studies of attrition rates for entering college freshmen and found that colleges lost approximately one half of their students in four years and that the attrition rate had not changed appreciably in forty years. Astin (1972) indicated that the greatest loss occurs between the freshman and sophomore years. More than one quarter of the freshmen at four-year schools and one third of the freshmen at two-year colleges fail to return for the next consecutive year.

College retention is a campuswide responsibility that begins with the admissions process. The admissions office sends out a variety of materials, answers inquiries, provides publications, visits high schools, and participates in college nights — all while exuding warmth and enthusiasm. Once the students are on campus, it becomes the responsibility of everyone else on campus to help to retain them. An effective academic advisement program will be the prime factor in increasing student retention during the 1980s and the 1990s. Academic advising assists students to achieve their optimal development by learning more about themselves, their aptitudes, and abilities and by utilizing the resources of their institution to attain their personal goals. Ramist (1981) recommends that institutions conduct their own research to determine the activities, characteristics, and programs that will bring about changes in institutional service that can enhance retention and eliminate factors that contribute to attrition.

Each campus must make a concentrated effort to develop a strategy to solve the problem of student retention. Expanding and improving advising services has already been mentioned. Retention can also be encouraged by upgrading and expanding the breadth of all services offered to students. Students who receive effective academic advising tend to feel positive not only about the advising process but about the institution as a whole (Noel, 1978). Academic advising is one of the most important roles that faculty perform, and the interaction between faculty and students is one of the most important factors in overcoming attrition. Good interaction fosters strong student satisfaction with college and increases self-perceived intellectual growth, self-esteem, and grades (Astin, 1977).

Academic Advising and Philosophy

It is not practical to identify one academic advising model as most suitable for all colleges, because each institution is unique in its characteristics, students, and faculty. Thus, each college should formulate its own philosophy, identify the available resources, determine the needs of its students, and evaluate its advising system periodically.

The school's commitment to academic advising is far more important than who actually does the advising on campus (O'Banion, 1972). Teague (1977) found that institutional recognition of the importance of advisement supersedes identification of either faculty or counselors as best qualified for the advising function. The institution's philosophy of advising is essential in establishing an advisement program. On our campus, the advising philosophy promotes individual attention. Students know that faculty members are genuinely concerned about them and that they can obtain any assistance that they need.

Our university utilizes a holistic approach in assessing not merely aptitude or academic achievement but the very real elements of personal needs and individual well-being. It utilizes the ACT test, which encourages students to conduct a thorough exploration of future plans, goals, and interests that are germane to the decision-making process. It is our obligation to recognize, integrate, and understand a student's personal evaluation of self, incorporating the aforementioned strengths, weaknesses, and desires and communicating this understanding systematically to the student. Once this has been done, our university must translate the programs and services to the student that are consistent with his self-exploration.

Our institutional philosophy on advising is that, as a state university with a basically open admissions policy, we must accept all students who graduate from New Mexico high schools. We must be sensitive to the needs, desires, and aspirations of these students. Students matriculate to a university for a variety of reasons, and the university has an obligation to assist students in identifying and fulfilling their goals. So, like most universities, we have developed a new interest in the nature of the student experience out of concern for retention. The academic advisor can be cast in uncomfortable roles, such as interpreting, defining, or enforcing rules and regulations. But the advisor should never overlook the wishes of the student totally in his concern for observing institutional regulations. He should do his best to see whether there are alternate ways of resolving conflicts that emerge.

Assignment of Advisers

On most college campuses that have no formalized student advisement program, student advising is generally conducted by assigning each new freshman to a particular faculty member. Sometimes, this assignment coincides with the student's major; many times, it has no relationship. At one institution where the author was employed, freshmen were assigned by the admissions office to each faculty member on the basis of an equal advisee load distribution. If Professor Jones had forty-three faculty advisees and Professor Smith had forty-two, the next student accepted was assigned to Professor Smith. At another institution, students were assigned to advisors on the basis of declared major. This can work very well, but it also has drawbacks. For example, in departments that have a lot of majors, an individual faculty member can have a disproportionate number of advisees.

Another disadvantage lies with the contacts between faculty member and student. Generally, the student must initiate contact. Many times when the student attempts to initiate contact, the faculty member is not available. When student and advisor do manage to get together, the sessions deal primarily with academic planning and course selection; little attention is given to other aspects of the student's academic life. Cummer (1961) found that satisfaction with advising was related to interested, available advisors who provided complete, accurate information and who had advisees from their own academic area.

Advising Records

Another major problem related to academic advising is the keeping of advising records. The institution, described in the previous section, that assigned advisees on an equal numerical basis kept advising records in the registrar's office, and advisors had no records with which to work. It is quite important for advisors to have a duplicate set of records on each student. These records should include such things as application forms, admission test scores, scores from any additional tests given for admission or placement purposes, high school and college transcripts, health records, and any additional correspondence or pertinent materials received in the admissions office. Many registrars are reluctant to provide this information, but they can retain the originals and create advising files that follow students through each year of the college program. These advising records can be expanded with additional test data, correspondence, college grades, and personal anecdotal records. It certainly helps if these records are kept in a central advising office and if there are regular hours and definite advising times for faculty advisors.

The Intrusive Approach

To be intrusive connotes a tendency to interest oneself in the affairs of others or to be unduly curious about another's concerns. The intrusive counseling and advising approach is based on the philosophy that institutions should not wait for students to get into trouble before they begin to give them advising or counseling. The intrusive system calls students for advising right from the beginning of the year and lets them know that there are people on campus who are concerned about them, who are interested in them, and who want them to succeed. During these intrusive sessions, advisors make students aware of the various support services that are available on the campus.

Intrusiveness is contradictory to the professional counseling approach, which maintains that counseling should be provided only when a student comes for help on his own initiative. In an academic setting, intrusive counseling is essential. Academic advisors provide information about or explanations of academic subjects, procedures, courses, and regulations. Advisors must provide accurate information, quick insight, and demonstrate good judgment. Dressel (1976) states that faculty advising systems are based on assumptions that faculty members are interested in students and knowledgeable about courses and graduation requirements and that students are receptive to advice. Academic advisors disseminate information, give advice, and provide services to students. They give talks to high school seniors who are prospective matriculants. They give orientation talks on admissions procedures. They assist students in selecting courses for the semester's work. They inform students about the requirements for specific majors. They verify graduation requirements and they provide information on possible study or work opportunities.

Use of faculty men and women as advisors makes the intrusive system work. Faculty advisors are given reduced time from their normal teaching load to assist in advising. The advising is conducted from a centralized advising center. These individuals are not trained counselors, and they need to be provided with an in-service program to assist them to become better advisors and counselors.

In-Service Training

Any advising system that does not train faculty members in the advising process works at a disadvantage. In many cases, advisors seem not to care whether they ever see a student or do any advising. On our campus, bimonthly meetings provide faculty advisors with information on the curriculum, college rules and regulations, and counseling techniques. These in-service sessions include guest speakers, such as counselor educators, psychologists, or student personnel workers from various elements of the university. Faculty advisors attend various national and state counseling and guidance conferences and workshops. They view counseling films and read counseling and educational and vocational guidance periodicals. They are instructed on the use of group guidance techniques for dissemination of information and on how to conduct case conferences on problem students.

Two Intrusive Models

University of Nevada, Las Vegas. The University of Nevada, Las Vegas (UNLV), is a state-supported institution with approximately 10,000 students. Its academic advising program was initially provided through the University College. Three years later, the advising program expanded under the jurisdiction of the vice-president of educational services, and a counseling, advising, and academic support system was developed.

The UNLV intrusive system includes eleven units: The University College is the college of record for all incoming freshmen and for undeclared sophomore majors. These students are advised by faculty members from each of the six upper-division colleges. The learning resource center provides tutoring and learning assistance and programmed materials to all students. The English as a Second Language program offers six levels of English courses to assist students from backgrounds in which a language other than English was the primary language. After students develop proficiency in English, they advance to regular academic majors. An early studies program offers outstanding high school juniors and seniors an opportunity to take college courses while they are still in high school. Admissions by alternative criteria gives students who cannot meet normal admissions requirements an opportunity to enter the university, take selected courses, and matriculate as regular students if they attain a C average. The psychological counseling and evaluation center has five clinical psychologists, who handle students' more severe personal, social, and emotional problems. Student affairs is responsible for student government, student activities, and the student union, and it provides peer counseling in the dormitory. Veterans' affairs handles advising and counseling for all veteran students. The placement and career center provides information on employment and career advising and coordinated interviews and job placement services. Special services provides advising, tutoring, and various services for physically, educationally, and culturally handicapped students. Finally, health services provides information, treatment, and diagnosis for health problems.

By unifying all these services, UNLV was ready to handle referrals, because all services were located in the same building. This move also promoted camaraderie among professional staff members in individual units. The students received better services from the university, and the various units did not have to compete to provide services or to receive credit, money, space, or additional personnel. Most college campuses have similar services, but unifying them and bringing them together in a team approach can make them more accessible and effective. On many campuses, units bicker and fight among themselves. As Clark Kerr (1972, p. 36) has stated, "The academic community is like the United Nations, with separate territories and cultures, veto powers, and the capacity for war. Coexistence is more likely than unity; peace is one priority item; progress another." Every campus element has its own turf, which it carefully guards. But the central administration must set the stage and coordinate the services campuswide. This was how UNLV coordinated its efforts.

By using the intrusive counseling model, UNLV reduced its freshman attrition rate from 45 percent to 5 percent over an eight-year period. It also reduced the number of students on academic probation and the number of withdrawals and academic suspensions, and it increased the number of students making the dean's list and the B honor roll and the overall student F.T.E. Fewer students dropped out of courses, and the number of freshmen requiring assistance from the psychological clinic declined (Glennen, 1972). This finding echoes that of Frank and Kirk (1975), who discovered that students who used the university counseling center had a lower dropout rate; as use of the counseling center increased, the dropout rate decreased.

Western New Mexico University. Western New Mexico University is a state regional university located in the southwest corner of New Mexico. It has an enrollment of 1,600 students, 46 percent of whom represent minorities. Western implemented its intrusive counseling program through a new unit called the General College. The General College is the college of record for all entering freshmen. Western's advising program was established to address the needs of high-risk students in a comprehensive, universitywide manner. The General College was created for the purpose of helping freshmen to achieve maximum success in the transition from high school to college. Freshmen do not have to declare a major, but they are required to complete requirements established by the upper-division colleges. When those requirements have been completed, students advance to one of the four traditional colleges: arts and letters, education, business and social science, or science and mathematics.

The specific responsibility of the General College is to provide a program of advising and guidance prior to and during the student's freshman year at Western. Under the direction of the college, students become acquainted with the educational opportunities of the university, and they are assisted in choosing a course of study most suitable to their own aptitudes and interests. Students have the advantage of taking courses in a variety of areas and the opportunity to investigate and explore academic interests before selecting a major. They are not required to declare a major until the end of their first year. Prior to that time, however, students are asked to state a planned major for the purpose of assigning an advisor and arranging a schedule. After their freshman year ends and they accumulate thirty-one credits, students declare a final choice of major and move to the upper-division college. If they are still undecided, they are allowed to remain in the General College until the end of the sophomore year (sixty-three credits).

As a state university with a basically open admissions policy, Western does not just process students, admit them to class, and take their money; it sees that they are provided with a real opportunity to acquire the career skills and education that they seek when they apply for admission. The college provides adequate and meaningful academic advising; accurate diagnosis of the level of academic skills, basic skills, and remedial services; career and psychological counseling; and integrated academic services to help all entering freshmen have a positive and successful learning experience.

Attrition and Advising. State of New Mexico enrollment statistics indicate that Western had a high freshman attrition rate for several years, ranging between 62 percent and 65 percent. The sophomore attrition rate ranged between 30 percent and 40 percent. These rates are extremely high when compared with national statistics. The attrition problem is being addressed through the advising program. Advisors are faculty members from the academic colleges. Advising takes place in a centralized location. Duplicate records are maintained on all students. These records are forwarded when the student advances to an upper-division college. Students know that between 8 A.M. and 5 P.M., Monday through Friday, someone is always available at the center to assist them with their problems. Every department that offers a major has a consultant to the General College. Consultants serve as backup to the normal advising system and answer questions that regular advisors cannot. The General College advisors provide advising, counseling, scheduling, and registration assistance. They review the file of each student advisee to learn more about academic records, test scores, family information, and physical and mental health and to identify any special problems that might hinder the learning process.

Support Components. The academic advising provided by faculty advisors is supplemented by professional counseling through the counseling center. The counseling center provides students with a wide variety of counseling services specifically designed to offer a strong support system to the student population at Western. These services include career and personal counseling, group counseling, administration and interpretation of tests, and diagnostic services.

The developmental skills center provides individual and group assistance in reading, writing, mathematics, and science. It administers the individual tutoring program. It provides learning materials, such as packaged programs, reading machines, audiovisual tapes, videotapes, and sound page materials, to increase the reading, writing, and comprehension skills of students. It also provides courses and materials on study skill improvement, learning techniques, note taking, listening skills, and use of the library.

The General College is responsible for the academic orientation of new freshmen, who are required to complete a testing program in addition to the ACT entrance requirement. The results of diagnostic tests are used to schedule students into their courses.

During the course of the semester, individual students are called in to the counseling and advisement office by means of a postcard. A second postcard is sent if the student does not respond within two weeks, and it is followed up by a phone call. If the student still has not reported by the end of one month, a letter is delivered by campus security. The postcard system has a 68 percent response rate, and the telephone follow-up picks up another 14 percent. Each faculty advisor spends six hours a week advising students and receives one three-credit course reduction from the normal teaching load. The criteria for both promotion and tenure include advising. The advisor's performance in the advising center is evaluated annually.

Each advisor is provided with an advising handbook that describes the recommended first-year program for each academic department that offers a major, the university's general education requirements, and other pertinent information, such as graduation requirements, financial aid requirements, student activities, counseling center services, and developmental skills services. The advisor is also provided with a university catalogue, a student handbook, and a reference manual indicating where to refer students. All students are assigned an advisor when they first report to the General College. The advisor comes from the student's area of intended major. The single most significant trait possessed by Western's academic advisors is their willingness to become involved with students in a close faculty–student relationship.

Outcome Measures. Although the intrusive program at Western New Mexico University is still in its infancy, it obtained some significant results in its first year of operation. For example, there was a record enrollment increase of 18.4 percent in the fall of 1982. The attrition rate for freshmen dropped from 66 percent in 1981 to 48 percent in the fall of 1982. Freshmen who enrolled in the fall of 1981, after the General College was put in place, enrolled for a significantly higher number of semester hours than students in 1980. Freshmen in the fall 1981 class had significantly higher completion rates of semester hours attempted than freshmen in the previous class. Freshmen enrolled had significantly higher mean grade point averages than freshmen in previous years. High semester hour load freshmen students achieved higher mean grade point averages and higher completion rates than freshmen enrolled prior to the creation of the General College. Higher semester hour loads did not adversely affect freshmen students' achievement as measured by grade point average and by completion rates of attempted hours. As measured by grade point average, achievement was higher for freshmen who enrolled for sixteen to twenty hours. The number of advising interviews increased from 595 in 1980–1981 to 792 in 1981–1982. Vocational and career counseling interviews increased from 106 in 1980–1981 to 383 in 1981–1982. The number of counseling contacts for all categories increased by 43.8 percent over the 1981–1982 year and by 96.9 percent from the level in 1979–1980, while tutoring contact hours increased from 476 in 1981 to 632 in 1982. The number of freshmen entering with an ACT composite score of ten or less who were still enrolled at the end of the semester increased from 71 percent in 1981 to 98 percent in 1982. The percentage of freshmen who completed the semester with honors increased, and the 87 percent who completed the year had an average grade point average of 2.27. Finally, personal and social counseling contacts decreased from 855 in 1980–1981 to 279 in 1981–1982.

Many interesting correlations exist between these findings and the results at UNLV. In his initial report on the intrusive advising process, Glennen (1972) indicated that faculty counselors at the University of Notre Dame had provided students with individual help and assisted freshmen in making a smooth transition from high school to college while reducing the freshman attrition rate to 1 percent at that highly selective, private university. Hutchins and Miller (1979) reduced attrition on their campus from the freshman and sophomore years by utilizing group interaction and by facilitating the faculty student advisement program. Their results indicated that there were fewer course and room changes, fewer disciplinary referrals and suspension, and less residence hall damage for the 144 students who went through the group process.

The Intrusive Sequence. The intrusive sequence at Western begins with the admissions process. The advising and counseling center receives a copy of the student's letter of acceptance, application form, and ACT results. At freshman orientation, the student is tested again, and data from the ACT and placement tests are used to schedule students into courses at the appropriate level. During the first three weeks of the academic year, students classified as marginal admissions — that is, students with a grade point average between 2.29 and 2.0 — are the first to be called in to the advising office. Throughout the course of the semester, the other students are called in at least once for a routine interview. The purpose of these interviews is to check on their academic progress on a course-by-course basis and to inform them of services that the university provides.

After midsemester exams, students who have two or more midterm deficiencies — D or F grades — are called in for additional counseling. These students are not threatened with suspension. Instead, advisors point out that whatever they have been doing up to that point in the semester has not worked, and they offer suggestions on how to improve their performance during the remainder of the semester. The last part of the fall semester is devoted to pre-registration for the spring semester.

At the beginning of the semester, new marginally admitted students are the first to be brought in, along with students on academic probation for poor performance during the fall semester. The next group of students to be seen by advisors are those who make the dean's list. These students are given personal congratulations, and interviews stress the various opportunities for honor students. Next, spring semester midterm deficiencies are called in, followed by preregistration for summer school and advance registration for the fall semester.

Another feature of the intrusive system at Western is advance registration for high school students. Faculty advisors visit high schools in the surrounding area in late April and early May and advance register students who are planning to attend Western. Students' schedules are placed on the computer, allowing students to know three months in advance what courses they will be taking and when the courses are scheduled and reserving space for them in the courses. Advance registration helps the university to know where additional sections of freshman-level courses will be needed.

The last step in the sequence of events at Western is forwarding of student files to the upper-division colleges at the conclusion of the second semester. An audit is done of students who have met requirements for advancing to upper-division colleges. When students' final grades are posted in the files, their folders move to the upper-division colleges so they will be on hand when the advising process begins as students enter their next academic year.

Throughout the course of the year, routine interviews are conducted with all students. There are readmission interviews for students dismissed in previous years, to determine whether they are ready to return to the university, and there are withdrawal interviews for students who plan to withdraw from the university. The purpose of withdrawal interviews is not to talk the student out of withdrawing but to determine the reasons and to assist the student to remain in school by providing solutions to the problem, such as financial aid, a part-time job, a reduction in course load, or referral to other specialized services. Another intrusive routine that continues throughout the year is trouble call-ins. Professors are encouraged to contact the advisement and counseling office if they notice that students are having academic problems, personal problems, or excessive absences. These students are called in. Many problems can be resolved before they become major.

Summary

The intrusive approach to student advising shares the basic elements of successful advising programs. Its philosophy reflects a genuine concern for each student as an individual, and the vehicle for providing advising and counseling is faculty-based. The intrusive approach provides faculty with in-service preparation and with tools of advisement, such as handbooks, catalogues, and referral sources, and it rewards them for successful advisement through monetary remuneration, promotion, and tenure. Further, the intrusive approach provides a centralized location where advising can take place in a confidential setting. It demands frequency and quality of advising contacts. It maintains comprehensive records, and it evaluates the outcome measures.

Intrusive advising has worked very effectively at several institutions. The author has been affiliated with three: University of Notre Dame, University of Nevada at Las Vegas, and Western New Mexico University. In addition, the author has served as a consultant to eighteen other colleges, universities, and community colleges in all regions of the country. These institutions that have adopted the intrusive approach have found that it is very effective on their campuses. Schrader (1980) studied the effects of intrusive counseling on freshman attrition and found that student satisfaction with advisors had a positive impact on student retention. Edington and Gilliard (1978) used the intrusive model to develop the Retention Advising Program (RAP) at Idaho State University with undecided students in the college of arts and letters. RAP was responsible for improving retention among those students.

With the demographics that institutions of higher education face in the next decade, intrusive advising and counseling might help to make up for declining enrollments. There will be a relative scarcity of college students over the next fifteen years. The competition in recruiting these students will be fierce. Colleges must provide assistance to retain the students who arrive on campus. Intrusive advising is a viable answer.

References

Astin, A. W. *College Dropouts: A National Profile.* Washington, D.C.: American Council on Education Research Reports, 7, 1, February, 1972.

Astin, A. W. *Four Critical Years: Effects of College on Beliefs, Attitudes, and Knowledge.* San Francisco: Jossey-Bass, 1977.

Breneman, D. W. *The Coming Enrollment Crisis.* Washington, D.C.: Association of Governing Boards, 1982.

"Carnegie Council's Final Report." *Chronicle of Higher Education,* 1980, *19* (19), 9-12.

Cummer, J. P. "Study of Counselor Satisfaction in Relation to Interest Level of Faculty Advisors in Counseling Activities." Unpublished doctoral dissertation, Florida State University, 1961.

Dressel, P. *Handbook of Academic Evaluation: Assessing Institutional Effectiveness, Student Progress, and Professional Performance for Decision Making in Higher Education.* San Francisco: Jossey-Bass, 1976.

Edington, R. V., and Gilliard, F. "R.A.P.: A Retention Advising Program." *Journal of College Student Personnel,* 1978, *19,* 472-473.

Frances, C. *College Enrollment Trends.* Washington, D.C.: American Council on Education, 1980.

Frank, A. C., and Kirk, B. A. "Differences in Outcomes for Users and Nonusers of University Counseling and Psychiatric Services." *Journal of Counseling Psychology,* 1975, *22,* 252–258.

Glennen, R. E. "Faculty Counseling: An Important and Effective Aspect of Student Development." *Research in Education,* 1972, *7* (4), 20.

Glennen, R. E. "Intrusive College Counseling." *College Student Journal,* 1975, *9* (1), 2–4, and *The School Counselor,* 1976, *24,* 48–52.

Hutchins, D. E., and Miller, W. B. "Group Interaction as a Vehicle to Facilitate Faculty-Student Advisement." *Journal of College Student Personnel,* 1979, *20,* 253–257.

Kerr, C. *The Uses of the University.* Cambridge, Mass.: Harvard University Press, 1972.

Noel, L. (Ed.). *Reducing the Dropout Rate.* New Directions for Student Services, no. 3. San Francisco: Jossey-Bass, 1978.

O'Banion, T. "An Academic Advising Model." *Junior College Journal,* 1972, *42,* 62–69.

Ramist, L. "College Student Attrition and Retention." *E.T.S. Findings,* 1981, *6,* 1–4.

Schrader, S. "Effects of Freshmen Intrusive Counseling Approach: Advisee Satisfaction and Reduction in Attrition." Unpublished doctoral dissertation, Ohio State University, 1980.

Summerskill, J. "Dropouts from College." In N. Sanford (Ed.), *The American College: A Psychological and Social Interpretation of the Higher Learning.* New York: Wiley, 1962.

Teague, G. V. "Community College Student Satisfaction with Four Types of Academic Advisement." *Journal of College Student Personnel,* 1977, *18,* 281–284.

Robert E. Glennen is president of Western New Mexico University in Silver City.

Open admissions in American higher education has resulted in
tremendous growth of learning centers. Centers provide
valuable assistance to underachieving students. Successful programs
are characterized by strong leadership, well-developed assessment and
placement processes, competence-based instruction, dedicated staff,
and program evaluation.

The Learning Center: A Study of Effectiveness

George A. Baker III
Percy L. Painter

College learning assistance programs, which range from full-fledged developmental studies programs to drop-in learning centers, are a relatively new phenomenon at colleges and universities. These centers are characterized by their emphasis on individualized instruction. They were necessitated by the emergence of a new, highly diverse clientele who responded to the invitation of open access to higher education during the 1960s. According to Cross (1976), in the 1950s, American higher education was characterized by an emphasis on academic excellence; thus, selective admissions were the rule. The 1960s were characterized by equal opportunity and open admissions, while the 1970s were characterized by faculty and instructional development in order to accommodate the shift in emphasis.

Cross (1976) believes that new challenges posed by accommodating the diversity of new students requires batch processing and group methods to be relinquished in favor of individualization. Students must be routed into self-paced and competence-based instruction. Instructional focus must shift from

The authors wish to acknowledge the leadership and assistance of James Hudgins, president of the Sumter Area Technical College. Without his commitment to student learning, the program documented in this chapter would not be exemplary.

J. E. Roueche (Ed.). *A New Look at Successful Programs.* New Directions
for College Learning Assistance, no. 11. San Francisco: Jossey-Bass, March 1983.

teacher-centered instruction to student-centered instruction. For program planners, teacher-controlled curriculum development must shift to specialized instruction for individual learners. To accommodate these challenges, many colleges developed college learning centers, developmental programs, and developmental courses. Devirian and others (1975) observed that 57 percent of all college learning centers became operative between 1970 and 1975. Sullivan (1980) reported that 1,778 learning center programs were in place on 1,374 campuses: Approximately one half of these centers were located on two-year college campuses.

Today, learning centers represent the most frequently employed campuswide program to assist students to be successful in academic endeavors (Beal, 1980). Leaders in the field of developmental education agree that the purpose of learning centers is to obviate the learning difficulties of students so they will be able to participate successfully in the core curriculum of the college. For students already enrolled in the core curriculum, learning centers often provide valuable assistance in negotiating the college curriculum (Matthews, 1981; Newton, 1982).

A number of forces present in the open-door college seem to indicate that learning centers make a significant contribution to student retention and to ultimate academic success. Major concerns addressed in open-door institutions center on issues relating to quality of instruction and to the cost of maintaining these aid stations for academic trauma. Despite these concerns, leveling enrollment, and increasing accountability, special policies and programs focused on student retention, appropriate literacy, and basic skills development are becoming ever more prevalent in American higher education (Roueche and Mink, 1980; McCabe, 1981). This chapter identifies the essential elements of learning centers dedicated to preparing students for the core curriculum. Successful programs are supported by strong leadership and well-developed assessment and placement models. Successful learning centers are characterized by instructional delivery systems, dedicated staffing, and program productivity. To illustrate how learning centers really work, the chapter includes a case study.

Assessment and Placement

The challenge of providing diverse instruction to diverse clients begins with assessment and placement based on policy analysis and no-nonsense student management. Policies and resulting decisions provide a safety net that yields a profile of student strengths and weaknesses and an accurate prediction of where the student needs to be placed in the academic sequence of courses in order to experience success. Although there are many assessment instruments relating to personality, attitudinal traits, and values, the key to proper academic placement resides in the area of basic cognitive skills. The primary focus of such testing is to assess the level of work that the student is ready to accomplish, not to determine whether the learner has the innate capacity to do the work.

The systematic context of the assessment program is perhaps the strongest factor in determining the success or failure of the learning center function and ultimately of the educational programs that comprise the college's core curriculum. No matter how well the assessment program is designed, it is useless unless the information that it yields allows accurate decisions to be made about student placement.

Instructional Delivery

The assessment process that yields an accurate picture of a student's strengths and weaknesses must be followed by instruction that is individualized, consistently evaluated, and revised to fit the needs of the learner and the institution. Cross (1976) believes that mastery learning techniques, including competence-based instruction, are the critical missing link in the education of low achievers. She argues that instruction must be both broken down into manageable units and individualized to fit the special needs of learners. Cross (1976, pp. 54–55) believes that five things are essential in developing success-oriented instruction for core curriculum–bound students: The student must be active rather than passive. The goals of learning must be clear, and they must be made explicit to students. Small lesson units are closely linked to course outcomes; they are desirable. Effective learning requires feedback evaluation. Finally, to recognize the tremendous individual differences in rate of learning, instructional systems must be self-paced, so the learner can control the pace of learning.

To increase student motivation, the content must be related to the learner's goals and needs. Although it may be difficult to personalize the specific tasks to be learned, the context in which the tasks are placed can certainly meet the test of relevance. In the instructional setting, student behavior must be managed in order to achieve successful results. Not only must instruction be systematically structured, but students who undertake such instruction often need structure in their thinking and subsequent behavior. Cross (1976) noted that the development of successful interpersonal skills is highly correlated with the exposure to highly structured academic programs.

Staffing

The first and perhaps most important staffing consideration in learning centers for core curriculum–bound students is that successful instructors have skills in delivering self-paced individualized instruction and a strong desire to work with students who require individualized help. Beyond these two selection prerequisites, Patterson (1980) argues for professional development to enhance prerequisite skills. In-service training is provided to foster understanding of the behavior of high-risk students, skills necessary for overcoming irresponsible behavior, willingness to accept responsibility for student learning, an understanding of instructional systems, and techniques that enable faculty to work with diverse students.

In order to form a powerful learning team, learning centers are typically staffed with counselors. Besides serving in the traditional therapeutic role, counselors assist students in managing their time and in making career choices. Counselors play a key role in student management and motivation. For example, at Miami–Dade Community College the role of the counselor is to support the learning process directly. Counselors there are considerably more directive than they are elsewhere. Since students are required to make acceptable progress in their academic pursuits, the role of the counselor becomes paramount (Schinoff, 1982). Such a philosophy of student management is supported by Moore (1976, p. 37), who states that high-risk students "want an advisor to make explicitly clear what is expected of them and what the consequences are for failure to follow certain institutional and faculty directions."

When they are well trained and supervised, paraprofessionals, tutors, and peer tutors can often fill other staffing roles necessary to ensure personalized attention and specialized help in individualized teaching and learning.

Program Management

Institutional response to the needs of underachieving learners has often been provided in the learning center format. However, research supports the notion that institutional response to underprepared learners is not a universal goal of higher education institutions with open admissions policies. As Spann (1977, p. 28) has noted, development programs often receive less support than other academic programs do as a result of "residual elitist attitudes" emanating from faculty who are often able to weaken the commitment of administrators who themselves may "lack a firm belief that the underprepared students also deserve a quality learning program."

In order to sustain the energy necessary to support a quality learning center for students who need help, institutional commitment must be visible. In fact, experts in the field of learning center format argue that administrative commitment is a prerequisite for success (Fisher, 1980; Garner, 1980). Generally, written policies are prerequisites to institutional commitment. Patterson (1980), who researched this relationship, has urged institutions to have written mission statements or other written policy oriented toward assisting underachieving students to succeed in college. In this regard, Roueche and Snow (1977) argue that, if the institution is willing to accept responsibility for meeting the needs of low-achieving students, program efforts assume a position of undergirding institutional objectives.

Productivity

Perhaps the most essential element in the learning center approach is an effective evaluation system designed to produce student success. Traditionally, when evaluation has been accomplished, it has served some external force, such as grant objectives or institutional research. Program evaluation for the sake of improving the quality of the academic program has seldom been seriously and persistently accomplished (Roueche and Roueche, 1977). Competence-based individualized instruction is particularly amenable to systematic evaluation, since learning outcomes are typically measurable (Herrscher and Watkins, 1980). When student learning is the focus, program evaluation can be accomplished by measuring students' persistence and achievement. When student persistence and achievement are measured, learning centers often focus on the reduction of educational obstacles. Evaluation efforts can be focused on both internal and external obstacles. According to Anderson (1980), internal obstacles include academic deficiencies, improper motivation, poor adjustment to college, low tolerance of frustration, self-doubt, career indecision, and fear of failure. External obstacles include lack of income, poor living arrangements, work demands, transportation problems, and social rejection. Since learning centers are established in order to deal with these problems, program evaluation should include schemes to ensure that both internal and external obstacles are reduced, controlled, or eliminated.

In the present economy, colleges should be able to demonstrate the cost-effectiveness of learning center programs. Since learning centers often are not fully funded from external sources, achievement gains and student persistence within the learning center and in core curriculum programs must be documented. When determining what to evaluate, college learning center leaders must be aware of the distinct differences between higher education and profit-making institutions. Millett (1975) makes a key distinction between businesses and colleges as social institutions: They operate in different contexts, and as a result they have different purposes. Business has the purpose of producing goods and services that produce a profit, while colleges have the purpose of promoting learning and advancing knowledge without producing a profit. In colleges, Millett notes, accountability measures are outcomes of the efforts of faculty members and their program leaders, not of administrators.

Since professionals must be self-motivated as a matter of professional pride to assume responsibility for program results and for plans to improve services for students, the focus of evaluation must relate to their achievements with students (Millett, 1975). Baldridge (1979) documents that colleges can practice modern management techniques within their unique contexts by balancing the relative needs of centralization and decentralization. Effective decision making should be placed at the lowest possible level, yet the program planning process must be linked to the budgeting process if continuing institutional support is to be expected. In the real world of management and administration, Baldridge concludes, shared power and conflict over resources have to be handled rather than hidden.

Learning center effectiveness must be measured not with evaluation models adopted from the profit sector but through a notion of productivity applicable to the business of teaching and learning. Hodgkinson (1981, p. 1) argues that educators who wrestle with issues of accountability, cost-effectiveness, and productivity "need to develop a notion of productivity that is compatible with the business we are in, not someone else's." The case study that follows deals with the issues of accountability for student learning, cost-effectiveness, and productivity in a community college setting. It documents how one institution over a period of several years has become accountable for student success.

Sumter Area Technical College: A Case Study

Sumter Area Technical College is an open-door institution that serves a four-county area of South Carolina. The median number of school years completed in the service area is 10.2. For students typically classified as disadvantaged, it is approximately 6.9 years. The college service area is experiencing a transition from an agrarian to an industrial economy. During that change, the college has grown from an education center with six full-time programs to a comprehensive college that serves more than 2,000 students through more than thirty-four academic programs.

The college's first learning center consisted of one small learning laboratory staffed by one full-time and one part-time instructor. Under this concept, students who were experiencing difficulty were referred for special help. The program grew and flourished and subsequently moved into the learning resources center of the college and expanded to serve the varying needs of students. Under the learning resources center concept, students were advised to undertake basic skills instruction on the basis of an analysis of test scores.

Individually Prescribed Instruction. During the 1973 academic year, the learning center adopted the Individually Prescribed Instruction (IPI) system developed by the Rehabilitation Research Foundation. The IPI system incorporated diagnostic testing and individual student learning prescriptions. Instructional strategies included the use of a large variety of commercially developed programmed materials. Instructional delivery included small sequences, with formative testing available as part of each instructional module.

In 1976, the Individualized Manpower Training System (IMTS) developed by Technical Education Research Centers was purchased for the learning center. The IMTS provided a well-structured student monitoring component that provided considerable amounts of instructional systems management information. Although the IMTS program had tremendous potential for meeting the needs of underprepared students, other centers were experiencing considerable difficulty in the open laboratory concept as a result of understructured staff and limited student control techniques.

After carefully evaluating the strengths and weaknesses of the IMTS, Sumter's learning center leadership accepted and adapted the system to meet local college needs. The college's early commitment to meet the special needs of its underprepared learners remained strong through stable and dedicated top-level leadership. The learning center approach at Sumter Area Technical College has experienced considerable success through experimentation and change over the past fourteen years. The overall approach in place today can be described as an umbrella concept that provides basic skills instruction and support in a developmental and transitional studies curriculum format to students who seek to attain college-level skills. This two-tiered approach provides basic skills and manages transition to curriculum-level programs.

Assessment and Placement. All students who choose a college-level program complete basic skills assessment tests. Counselor analysis of test scores leads to placement in entry-level courses for which management information system data predict a high probability of academic success. Students who need to acquire basic skills are assigned to basic skills or to transitional course sequences and to a faculty adviser who is responsible for monitoring their progress and for providing a human support system.

The key to success for the assessment and placement component has been the coordinated effort between curriculum and learning center decision makers. Curriculum decision makers established entrance and exit competencies for entry-level curriculum courses in reading, mathematics, and English. Entrance and exit competencies were then correlated with appropriate entry-level placement test scores. These scores are shared with students as a means of increasing their information about institutional expectations of increased competence. Once competencies in the basic skills areas have been determined and expected test score levels have been established, decision makers in the academic areas and learning center collaborate to determine and design the sequence and content of basic skills courses necessary to bridge the gap between developmental lab and curriculum courses. The transitional sequences include three mathematics, two English, four reading, and five science courses.

Organization and Decision Making. Certain key elements must be in place in order to serve underdeveloped students. One overriding aspect is organization of the learning center and the decision making involving students and their progress at Sumter Area Technical College. The developmental needs of students were gradually conceptualized as a transitional period leading to college-level work. Over a period of fourteen years, the effort at Sumter grew from a one-room learning laboratory, to departmental status, and then to divisional status as the college continued to respond to the unique needs of the students and the community. As the effort grew, the division expanded to include special services, the college testing center, and all the college's general studies departments.

Organization of general studies and basic skills instruction as a single division occurred as a result of the college's commitment to a competence-based instructional approach that encompassed a continuum from entry-level to exit-level skills in the basics of reading, writing, and mathematics. In the first stages of implementing collegewide competence-based instruction, each program worked with its advisory committee to update program exit competencies. The college's instructional specialist met with each program faculty and with faculty in related areas to ensure that all program competencies would be included for student mastery. Subsequently, entry-level competencies were developed, and placement criteria were set for each program.

Transitional Studies. In order to respond to the educational needs of underprepared students, the transitional studies program provides them with an opportunity to reach their academic goals in a variety of settings. The umbrella approach, depicted in Figure 1, encompasses industry, adult education, developmental studies labs, general education development, and preparatory programs. All have developed competence-based instruction as well as

Figure 1. Transitional Studies

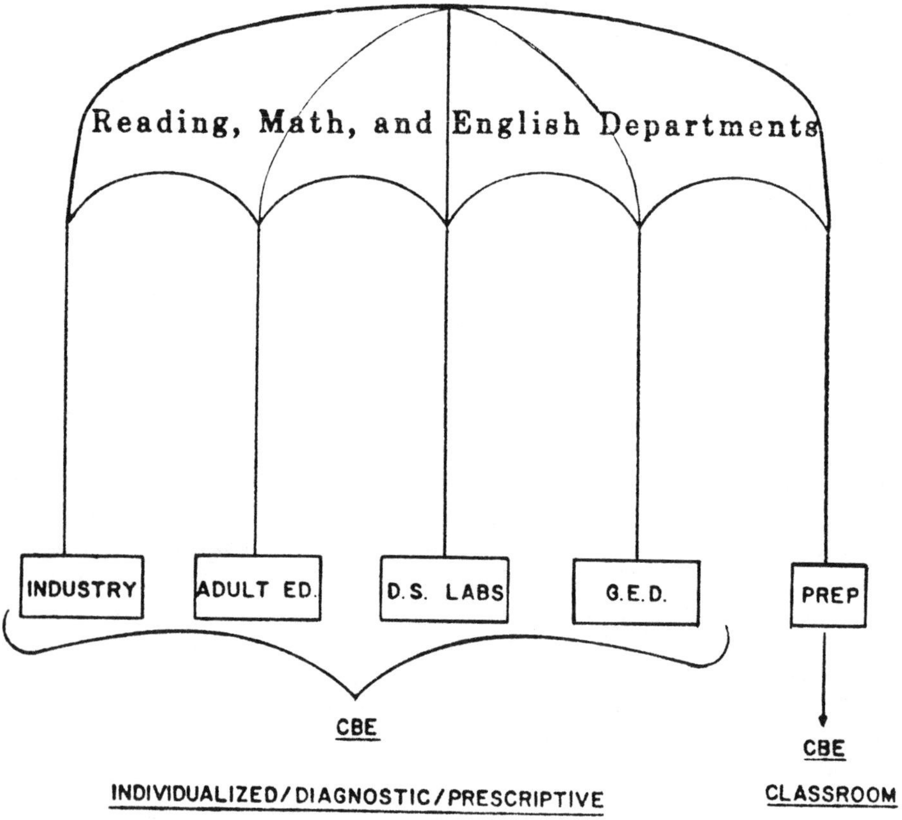

Reading, Math, and English Departments

INDUSTRY ADULT ED. D.S. LABS G.E.D. PREP

CBE

INDIVIDUALIZED/DIAGNOSTIC/PRESCRIPTIVE

CBE

CLASSROOM

individualized diagnostic-prescriptive curricula. Through cooperative efforts with three industrial sites, programs have been established on plant sites to respond to individuals who find it difficult to attend instruction on the main campus.

The preparatory program (PREP) was implemented in fall 1981 so that the curriculum programs could fully implement competence-based instruction after completing competence analysis and setting program goals. PREP objectives were designed to provide a transition phase for students between the developmental lab setting, to provide an intensive advisement for high-risk students, to balance course loads with outside commitments, and to alleviate the overcrowded conditions in the developmental studies lab.

A coordinated effort between curriculum and developmental department heads was undertaken in order to establish entrance and exit competencies for entry-level curriculum courses. These entrance competencies, which were translated into college entrance placement test scores, were designed to help students reach the exit competencies stated in program goals. Once these decisions had been made, general studies and transitional studies department heads worked together to determine the number and content of courses needed to bridge the gap between developmental lab individualized courses and curriculum courses. This group of transitional developmental courses, known as the preparatory program, included three mathematics, two English, four reading, and five science courses.

Students directed to PREP have not met the entrance criteria for their programs, and they must complete PREP work successfully before they are fully accepted. PREP faculty adviser-advisee loads have been reduced, so that advisers can spend extra time monitoring the PREP student's progress and make fast referrals to any needed support service. PREP advisers work closely with curriculum department heads to determine which courses students should take while still in PREP status. Once a student has completed all PREP courses successfully, the student is admitted to a program and assigned to a curriculum adviser.

Advising and Counseling Component. Since the typical student faces a reduced chance of success, it is imperative to establish an aggressive counseling component. The counseling component provides an early alert system as well as constant monitoring of the student by department and primary group advisers. The contacts made by advisers on a continuous basis assure the student of the program's concern while advisers work with the student to confirm goals and to manage the time available for learning.

To form the counseling component, the transitional studies department heads were assigned to sections as faculty advisers, and each learning manager was assigned to be primary adviser for a specific group. These two advisers worked closely together, as well as with all other learning managers, to provide a coordinated personal monitoring system that would keep the program personalized and responsive to student needs. The faculty adviser, a transitional studies department head, became the program's initial contact with the student. The faculty adviser registered and scheduled the student to a manageable time frame. Extensive orientation was conducted by faculty advisers and primary advisers. It related to all lab procedures, and it introduced the student to the resources and services available at the college. The primary adviser has a converence with each assigned student at the beginning of each quarter. The student completes a personal data form and produces an individualized study schedule. In order to reinforce the relevance of the study schedule, the learning manager reviews an analysis of basic skills competencies to be mastered, indicates areas in which special effort will be required, and relates the deficient competencies to chosen curriculum goals.

An advisement seminar is led by the faculty adviser in order to provide the student with an opportunity to work with both advisers. The student receives information about the student's current achievement level and about what the student must achieve in order to enter and succeed in achieving academic goals. Tours of curriculum programs are scheduled to provide students with an opportunity to visit classrooms and shops. Curriculum department heads instruct students regarding their chosen career goals and the employment outlook in that field of endeavor. This orientation provides the students with an opportunity to look at their chosen career area, as well as other options, and to have personal contact with a faculty member in that area.

Student Management System. The advising and counseling component of the program is designed to structure the developmental program in its entirety, allowing students to experience academic success and enter their chosen curriculum program. Thus, a management system is of paramount importance. Effective management is essential in increasing efficiency and improving program operations. Effective management in an educational setting depends on the availability of needed information. Management information at Sumter Area Technical College involves three distinct levels: management of student progress, management of staff performance, and management of the instructional system itself.

Management of Student Progress. The student's commitment to a time schedule is established by using a block scheduling procedure to assign students to individual labs for a given number of hours a week. Students are assigned to particular sections. Each section is subdivided into three groups. This arrangement establishes teacher accountability for the fifteen students in each section.

Grading and attendance policies are based on the premise that regular attendance is necessary in order for students to be successful in future endeavors. The college's attendance policy, which includes notifying students early in the quarter of possible attendance problems, provides for conferences between learning managers and students to discuss attendance problems and to develop attendance contracts.

The grading system is compatible with competence-based instruction, as mandated by college policy. Students are able to earn letter grades of A, B, C, D, or F. A point system establishes the standards for each grade. Students earn a fixed number of points for passing each module with a grade of 85 percent or better. Increased points are awarded to students who pass tests on the first attempt. The use of bonus points motivates students to study effectively and efficiently. By providing students with the structure to pace themselves in their courses, this grading system overcomes one limitation of traditional self-paced instruction. Students are assigned work only on their own grade level. They are not expected to compete with other students for a grade. The learning manager assigns alternate instructional materials to students who demonstrate that they cannot handle a particular assignment.

To coordinate all efforts into a unified management structure, learning managers participate in linear management meetings. Each subject matter instructor meets at a regularly scheduled time to discuss the progress of students. For each student, six topics are the focus of the meeting: information recorded on the student's personal data form; the student's daily attendance record in each class; the number of times when the student has been late for class; the number of points that the student has accumulated in each subject; the student's effectiveness in using instructional time, as determined by comparing the amount of time spent in class to the amount of time spent on task; and the student's effectiveness in studying, as determined by comparing the total number of tests that the student has taken with the number of tests that the student has passed. These meetings enable the learning managers to update student progress and to share concerns and successes. Linear management meetings form the nucleus of the management system and ensure a holistic approach to student development. Counseling sessions, modifications of the study schedule, and changes in written student contracts play a vital role in student management and are often the natural consequence of information gathered at management meetings. Student contracts and progress folders are used to motivate and encourage students to become more efficient, effective, and independent learners.

Management of Staff Performance. Staff management is imperative, since the system's entire success depends on the competencies of learning managers and on the personal interaction provided by them to students. Commitment to a fifteen-to-one student-to-teacher ratio as well as monetary limitations necessitated the use of paraprofessionals as learning managers. To guarantee instructional development and content validity, a department head in each academic skill area provides leadership. Extensive staff training is provided by the department heads, not only when learning managers are employed but also on a scheduled daily basis throughout employment within the division.

Learning managers are evaluated quarterly. A competence-based system developed by the learning managers themselves is used. The department heads serve as curricula specialists and critique each study schedule prepared by learning managers. The department head is the facilitator at each management meeting. All other department heads attend. Continual staff training occurs at these meetings, since decisions involve students who experience problems that call for represcribing, a conference with the student, or changing a contract made by the student.

Management of the Instructional System. Program management is essential to ensure accountability in the developmental program. Record keeping provides a data base that facilitates student and program evaluation and management. Student evaluation of the program is given major consideration. The program's philosophy serves as the foundation for all management decisions. It was developed by the transitional studies division dean and department heads together with the South Carolina technical education coordinator for developmental education. Accountability for program productivity encompasses product evaluation as well as process evaluation. Articulation and feedback from all departments of the college are necessary to educate the rest of the college about the ways in which developmental education can be of service to them. Administrative support is a must. Therefore, it is important to keep the college administration fully informed of program accomplishments as well as of all other aspects of the program. Seeking the involvement of administration has had the effect of improving instruction in all aspects of the institution.

Productivity at Sumter Area Technical College. As stated earlier in this chapter, colleges typically do not evaluate their programs well, since data on how much students learn is not often available. Sumter Area Technical College overcame this problem by developing an institutional competence-based instruction program. In the learning center effort, management decisions have become data-driven, since information about student progress as measured by modules completed and grade levels of basic skills gained through the curriculum process is available. Thus, the college has been able to focus decision making on the two key outcome variables not typically available in instructional program evaluation: persistence and achievement.

With adoption of the IMTS in 1976, division leadership was able to collect data and evaluate one key aspect of the division's overall productivity. Evaluation translated into the research question, How many hours of student persistence and study are required to cause students to progress one grade level? During the fall quarter of the three school years between 1977 and 1979, a careful research study was completed. The results are displayed in Table 1.

Table 1 shows that learning managers at Sumter were able to improve their efficiency in assisting students to attain basic skills competencies between the initial evaluation conducted in fall 1977 to the evaluation conducted in fall 1979. Efficiency improved by 11 percent in reading, by 20 percent in math, and by 44 percent in English instruction. Since student achievement data were available at the end of each quarter, the division was able to make necessary improvements on a quarterly basis.

While the research conducted between 1977 and 1979 demonstrated that the college could be efficient in helping students to master basic skills

Table 1. Basic Skills Achievement

Subject	Fall 1977	Fall 1978	Fall 1979	Two-Year Gain
Reading				
Students	81	66	66	
Hours	28	31	25	11%
Math				
Students	58	65	65	
Hours	35	30	28	20%
English				
Students	50	65	65	
Hours	45	28	25	44%

Note: Hours = instructional time necessary for the average student to progress one grade level on the appropriate achievement test.

content, it did not answer the question, Do high-risk students assigned to basic skills instruction achieve in a fashion comparable with students whose test scores indicate that they do not need special preparation? During 1980, a research study was conducted to determine whether there were significant differences between groups of students who completed developmental work and students who qualified to enter the program of their choice in other ways. After carefully controlling for such variables as curriculum choice, age, sex, and reading level, the researcher concluded that there were no significant differences between the grade point averages of the two groups. During 1981 and 1982, approximately one fourth of the graduates of the college enrolled in one or more areas of basic skills instruction, and no discernable differences were apparent in persistence and achievement between those who did and those who did not receive basic skills instruction at the college.

Such data answer two key questions about the productivity of the learning center. Data collected in the Sumter program indicated that students were learning basic skills competencies and that in subsequent programs they performed in a similar fashion to those who met program entry requirements. It is clear that such data document a productive program. However, two other questions remain unanswered: What does the program cost? Do students complete the program successfully? Table 2 presents cost data relating to staff necessary to conduct the program. The data include all personnel directly assigned to work with students. Overhead costs, such as administration and instructional materials, are not included, but they are comparable to costs in other divisions of the college.

Table 2 displays cost per credit hour and retention data for three fall quarters. Between 1977 and 1979, staff cost tripled, while the number of students served increased from 164 in 1977 to 384 in 1979. Credit hours earned doubled, from 3,372 in 1977 to 6,480 in 1979. The cost per credit hour of instruction ranged between $4.38 in 1977 and $8.60 in 1978. In 1979, the cost per credit hour dropped to $6.96. Employing an average cost per credit hour

Table 2. Cost, Credit, and Retention Data, 1977–1979

	Fall Quarter 1977	Fall Quarter 1978	Fall Quarter 1979
Department Heads	$ 8,917.06	$10,276.69	$11,824.31
Associate Teachers	4,304.40	8,449.25	9,993.16
Assistant Teachers	1,566.00	21,669.82	20,515.70
Clerk		1,388.29	2,795.04
Total Staff Cost	$14,787.46	$41,784.05	$45,128.21
Total Enrollment	164	237	384
Credit Hours Earned	3,372	4,854	6,480
Cost per Credit Hour	$ 4.38	$ 8.60	$ 6.96
Retention Rate (Percent of Students Completing the Quarter)	67%	78%	84%

of $6.92, we find that the developmental effort compares favorably with all academic programs of the college, and that it costs considerably less than most college settings. The data most indicative of the program's productivity relate to the retention rate. The program retained 67 percent of the students in 1977, with 45 percent of the students enrolled earning at least one F or D. In 1978, the retention rate increased to 78 percent, and only 19 percent of the students enrolled earned a negative grade. By 1979, the center was retaining 84 percent of the students enrolled, with 28 percent earning at least one negative grade.

Summary. The developmental program at Sumter Area Technical College joins a small minority of colleges in America that have made a commitment to high-risk students. Instructional support systems, such as mandatory assessment and placement and a counseling component dedicated to student development and success, are in place. Instructional systems employ competence-based curriculum development and individualized self-paced learning laboratory processes. Staff are selected for their professional competence and their commitment to the goals of the institution, and they receive training to help them work with high-risk students. Program management data, including data on student academic progress and student management, become the basis for decision making that is decentralized to the level where it is reasonable to expect accountability for student learning. Finally, college and program leadership continually cause research to be completed to determine the program's productivity. Student achievement, academic success, cost data, and retention figures are available, and institutional and program decision making is data-based. The transitional studies division and its developmental program at Sumter Area Technical College truly show program effectiveness.

References

Anderson, E. "Promoting Persistence and Academic Achievement Among Minority Undergraduates Based on a Force Field Analysis of Student Adjustment." Paper presented at University of California, Los Angeles, April 1980.

Baldridge, J. "Impacts on College Administration." *Research in Higher Education,* 1979, *10,* 263–282.

Beal, P. E. "Learning Centers and Retention." In O. T. Lenning and R. L. Nayman (Eds.), *New Roles for Learning Assistance.* New Directions for College Learning Assistance, no. 2. San Francisco: Jossey-Bass, 1980.

Cross, K. P. *Accent on Learning: Improving Instruction and Reshaping the Curriculum.* San Francsico: Jossey-Bass, 1976.

Devirian, M. C., Enright, G., and Smith, G. D. "Survey of Learning Programs in Higher Education." In *Twenty-Fourth Yearbook of the National Reading Conference.* Clemson, S.C.: National Reading Conference, 1975.

Fisher, J. L. "The President and the Professionals." In J. L. Fisher (Ed.), *Presidential Leadership in Advancement Activities.* New Directions for Institutional Advancement, no. 8. San Francisco: Jossey-Bass, 1980.

Garner, A. "A Comprehensive Community College Model for Learning Assistance Centers." In K. V. Lauridsen (Ed.), *Examining the Scope of Learning Centers.* New Directions for College Learning Assistance, no. 1. San Francisco: Jossey-Bass, 1 9 8 0 .

Herrscher, B. R., and Watkins, K. *Competency-Based Education: An Overview.* New York: HBJ Media Systems, 1980.

Hodgkinson, H. L. "Moving Beyond Productivity to Quality." *AAHE Bulletin,* 1981, *33* 1–3.

McCabe, R. H. "Now Is the Time to Reform the American Community College." *Community and Junior College Journal,* May 1981, *51* (8), 6–10.

Matthews, J. M. "Becoming Professional in College-Level Learning Assistance." In F. L. Christ and M. Coda-Messerle (Eds.), *Staff Development for Learning Support Systems.* New Directions for College Learning Assistance, no. 4. San Francisco: Jossey-Bass, 1981.

Millett, J. D. "Higher Education Management Versus Business Management." *Educational Record,* 1975, *56,* 221–225.

Moore, W., Jr. *Community College Response to the High-Risk Student: A Critical Reappraisal.* Washington, D.C.: AACJC, 1976 (ED 122 873).

Newton, E. S. *The Case for Improved College Teaching: Instructing High-Risk College Students.* New York: Vantage Press, 1982.

Patterson, M. C. M. "A Study of Congruence Between Delphi-Validated Policies and Procedures Which Promote Learning Among High-Risk Students and Current Practices in Selected Community Colleges." Unpublished doctoral dissertation, University of Texas, Austin, 1980.

Roueche, J. E., with Mink, O. G. *Holistic Literacy in College Teaching.* New York: Media Systems, 1980.

Roueche, J. E., and Roueche, S. D. *Developmental Education: A Primer for Program Development and Evaluation.* Atlanta: Southern Regional Education Board, 1977.

Roueche, J. E., and Snow, J. J. *Overcoming Learning Problems: A Guide to Developmental Education in College.* San Francisco: Jossey-Bass, 1977.

Schinoff, R. B. "No Nonsense at Miami–Dade." *Community and Junior College Journal,* November 1982, *53* (3), 34–35, 44.

Spann, M. G. "Building a Developmental Education Program." In J. E. Roueche (Ed.), *Increasing Basic Skills by Developmental Studies.* New Directions in Higher Education, no. 20. San Francisco: Jossey-Bass, 1977.

Sullivan, L. L. "Growth and Influence of the Learning Center Movement." In K. V. Lauridson (Ed.), *Examining the Scope of Learning Centers.* New Directions for College Learning Assistance, no. 1. San Francisco: Jossey-Bass, 1980.

George A. Baker III is executive director of the National Institute for Staff and Organizational Development. He teaches in the Community College Leadership Program at the University of Texas, Austin.

Percy L. Painter is division dean of instructional services and general studies at Sumter Area Technical College, South Carolina and past president of the South Carolina Technical Education Association.

*Evaluating the costs as well as the outcomes of developmental
programs can increase institutional acceptance and support,
while ensuring accountability for institutional resources.*

Adding Up the Numbers: Assessing Program Costs and Outcomes

Mary Stubbs

Evaluating program costs and outcomes can strike fear into the hearts of developmental educators. We want to make it known that our programs are complex, that the number of variables to be considered is amost infinite, and that the way we effect change in student's lives is subtle, although significant. In this context, we describe the dangers inherent in simply adding up numbers. All these points are valid as they stand. They become invalid, however, when we add *Therefore, we cannot quantify the costs and outcomes of such programs.*

In recent years, a significant number of research studies have shown that developmental programs contribute to a successful college experience for high-risk students (Friedlander, 1981–1982). However, the question that continues to surface is, At what cost? Since resources are limited, should community colleges offer developmental programs for academically underprepared students, or should these resources be allocated to programs that are more cost-effective? Providing answers to these questions is the best and most immediate justification for ongoing evaluation of costs and outcomes of developmental programs. At Westmoreland County Community College (WCCC), we have answered these questions. In 1979, a local consulting firm was hired to evaluate our developmental studies program. Through retrospective com-

J. E. Roueche (Ed.). *A New Look at Successful Programs.* New Directions
for College Learning Assistance, no. 11. San Francisco: Jossey-Bass, March 1983.

parative analysis, the consultant determined that WCCC developmental program students were significantly more successful across all measures of academic performance than underprepared students who bypassed the program and that the program was a net income generator for the college.

The Setting

WCCC is a relatively small, rural community college in southwestern Pennsylvania with a current enrollment of 3,241 students, 60 percent of whom attend classes part-time. Women students constitute a slight majority. The average student age is twenty-eight. Most students are the first in their families to attend college. WCCC offers a liberal arts associate degree program and twenty-one occupational programs, with a variety of program options to accommodate students' educational and employment goals and interests. Sponsored by the county, the college enrolled its first students in January 1971. Currently, there are fifty-one full-time faculty and a large contingent of part-time faculty, particularly in the occupational programs. A commitment to developmental education has existed at WCCC from its beginning as a requisite instructional component in an open-door institution. In the early years, developmental courses in English, reading, and mathematics were offered as lecture-recitation classes in a traditional classroom setting. In 1975, we began the process of reviewing student performance in courses subsequent to students' participation in developmental courses. Several consultants were engaged, who, through faculty questionnaires, discussion, and review of available data, offered recommendations for change in order to develop a more effective learning experience for students and better continuity between developmental courses and subsequent courses. With this information and with ideas gathered from the literature on developmental education, a comprehensive developmental studies program was introduced in the fall 1975 semester as an individualized, self-paced, competence-based program.

Program Design

From the outset, the program included a strong evaluation component to verify that the program design was appropriate to accomplish the goal of preparing academically disadvantaged students for success in college programs. Processes were developed to collect and organize information about developmental students on entry, during their developmental courses, and after the developmental experience. Minor revisions in the data-gathering processes have taken place; however, the processes and questionnaires remain essentially the same.

WCCC uses the Comparative Guidance and Placement Test to identify students who need improvement in writing, reading, and mathematics. Students who score below established cutoff points are required to take developmental courses. At present, an ad hoc committee is reviewing the college's placement testing procedures to determine whether the test and cutoff scores currently used continue to be appropriate and useful. At present, the developmental reading course is not required. This policy is also under review.

The developmental studies program operates as an individual unit of the division of learning resources. Its own budget provides for all direct costs. The program is staffed with three full-time faculty, three full-time instructional assistants, a counselor, and a clerk. Initially, only the faculty positions were funded by the college budget; after several years, the instructional assistants and the clerk were absorbed by the college budget, and the counselor continues to be externally funded. Professional tutors, who have at least a bachelor's degree, are hired as needed. Peer tutors are not used in the program.

Students learn in a variety of modes in this program. Audiovisual materials are used as well as cassette-work book combinations, work sheets, and modules designed by the staff. Instruction is provided on a one-to-one basis, with a maximum of sixteen students in each of the three areas — writing, mathematics, and reading and study skills — at any one time. Students must achieve 80 percent mastery of the course content for exit. While all students are required to spend three hours per week per course, those who are particularly deficient are encouraged to spend additional hours each week.

Initially, credit earned for developmental courses could not be used to meet degree requirements. Several years ago, college policy was changed to allow students to use developmental courses as general electives in all programs except liberal arts and nursing. Students who complete developmental courses earn three credits per course and receive the grade of CR (credit). The grade of I (incomplete) is given to students who are close to completing a developmental course at the end of the semester; they are permitted to register for sequential courses in the next semester, but they must complete the developmental work usually within the first thirty days of the following semester. These students also are given the opportunity to work toward completion of a developmental course between semesters. However, a significant number of students cannot achieve the exit requirement of 80 percent mastery in one semester. Provided that these students are attending regularly and that they are making progress, they receive the grade of IP (in progress) at the end of the semester. Students who receive the IP grade are required to register for the course for the next semester.

The developmental studies program operates in a space called the Learning Lab, which includes instructional space as well as faculty and counselor offices. An in-depth orientation is provided for all students in developmental courses to explain the instructional methods, the course objectives, and faculty expectations and to familiarize students with the learning lab environment, staff, and services.

Each student who enters the lab completes a master file form, which includes the usual demographic data together with information on career goals,

92

family responsibilities, hours worked each week, a personal assessment of the student's high school experience, placement test scores, the student's schedule of classes, and a self-descriptive paragraph that begins with the words *I am.*

During the first few weeks of the semester, the developmental studies counselor has a brief interview with each student. As entering students complete their master file, files are given to the counselor, who thus has a fairly detailed profile of each student prior to the initial interview. The primary purpose of these interviews is to make students aware of the counselor's presence and by initiating the first contact to overcome students' hesitance or reluctance to initiate contact with a counselor.

Just beyond midsemester, each student completes a questionnaire evaluating his or her experience in the developmental studies program. As each semester is completed, the college data center provides printouts showing students enrolled in developmental courses and listing subsequent courses taken and grades earned.

Because of regular assessment of student data on performance in developmental studies and in courses and students' evaluations of their experience, the developmental program staff felt confident that the program was working well, that it was meeting the needs of students, and that it supported college efforts to maintain academic standards by ensuring that students developed the skills needed for success in college-level work. But, as in many institutions, two nagging questions persisted: Do students do better for having taken developmental courses? What does it cost?

Program Evaluation

In spring 1979, the president of WCCC decided that an in-depth evaluation of the developmental studies program should be conducted by someone outside the college, and a consultant was selected and hired by the board of trustees. Each academic division was asked to provide the consultant with its questions about the developmental studies program. A long list of questions emerged. Most divisions asked essentially the same question: Can we identify a difference in student academic performance that we can attribute to developmental courses? Some divisions questioned the practice of allowing students more than one semester to complete developmental courses.

The second major concern that emerged focused on cost. Although we had regularly gathered and analyzed data on student performance, we had not studied program costs. For several reasons, most faculty and staff assumed that developmental studies was a high-cost program. In 1979, much of the literature regarding developmental programs either ignored the cost issue or suggested that such programs were worthwhile although costly. It was suggested that, compared with other, more traditional instructional modes, our program structure could not be cost-effective. Each member of the developmental studies faculty has a full-time instructional assistant, and students are scheduled in relatively small numbers (a maximum of sixteen at one time); in regular courses, class size is twenty-five students or more, and there are no instructional assistants.

The Consultant's Approach. Having identified the questions and concerns regarding developmental studies, the consultant specified his objective as "to quantify the WCCC Developmental Program's impact on the WCCC student, the college, and the community through the use of retrospective comparative analyses" (Cicco and Associates, 1979, p. 3). The study included data on all students from fall 1975 through spring 1979 who scored below established cutoff points on the Comparative Guidance and Placement Test. Students in this group were then divided into those who completed the developmental courses for which placement scores indicated a need and those whose scores indicated a need for such courses but who did not take developmental courses. Persistence, grade point averages, and program completion were compared for students in these two groups. During summer 1978, the three-person consultant team gathered data throughout the college. The findings and the report document were presented to the assembled faculty and administration at the start of the fall semester.

Evaluation Results. The consultant's assessment showed that academically underprepared students who took developmental courses earned a quality point average (QPA) 18 percent higher than underprepared students who did not take developmental courses. Developmental takers, as they came to be known during the study, had a 32 percent better graduation rate and a 34 percent longer enrollment rate at the college than nontakers did. Utilizing data gathered over four years of student course evaluations, the consultant reported that 86 percent of the developmental program students believed that developmental courses had significantly improved their chances to complete academic programs. Thus, the college received a definitive and affirmative answer to one question: The developmental studies program clearly makes a difference in achieving academic success for underprepared students.

The second area of analysis focuses on the ways in which the developmental studies program benefited the college. The consultant found that, excluding credits earned in developmental courses, developmental takers accrued 30 percent more credits than nontakers — and 43 percent more if their developmental course work was included.

A thorough analysis of program costs determined that, from its inception in 1975, the developmental studies program had provided $387,220 in revenues, which, when balanced against $241,449 in direct costs, resulted in a net income of $145,771 and provided a 60.4 percent return on expenses. Although data on indirect costs were not available, the consultant observed that, even if indirect costs reached 60 percent of direct costs, the program would still be an income generator, not a drain on institutional resources.

The consultant reported the following effect of retention of developmental students on college income (Cicco and Associates, 1979, p. 1): "Also, the increased retention of the developmental students has helped provide an additional $208,787 in revenues over the past four years, and an estimated $336,335 may have been lost due to the lack of improved retention from those underprepared students who bypassed the prescribed developmental work during the same period."

As the college is sponsored by the county through its commissioners, the consultant attempted to identify ways in which the developmental program benefited the larger community. The student course evaluation form includes the statement "I feel that taking this developmental course is useful to me in my daily life outside the college." Sixty-five percent of the students said that they agreed strongly or agreed somewhat with this statement; only 11 percent disagreed.

The consultant also analyzed employment data gathered through regular surveys of graduates and found that, among graduates employed in positions for which they were educated at WCCC, only 32.1 percent of the developmental program students had left Westmoreland County, compared with 48.5 percent of the nontakers. With the caveat that the nature of the data precludes definitive conclusions, the consultant observed (Cicco and Associates, 1979, p. 16) that "it does appear that there may be a tendency for the developmental course participant's increased involvement with the college to translate, after graduation, to a generally stronger tie to the county itself."

Evaluation Impact. By confirming the cost-effectiveness of the WCCC program, the study created a more positive environment in the institution for developmental studies. The administration was reassured by the knowledge that the program is a financial asset, not a liability, and faculty and staff showed a new confidence in the program as an effective means of improving the academic performance of underprepared students. Of course, it was a powerful morale builder for developmental program staff.

Factors Affecting the Study

A number of factors contributed to the feasibility of the program evaluation study. Certainly, the most important factor was that extensive data were available because the program had included a carefully designed evaluation component from its inception in 1975. Also, institutional practices made it possible to identify two groups of academically underprepared students that could serve as a control group and an experimental group. Although the developmental studies program proposal provided that students who scored below established cutoff points on the Comparative Guidance and Placement Test would enroll in developmental courses, many students managed to bypass the placement process, thus creating the group identified in the study as nontakers.

Since the evaluation report was completed in 1979, the loopholes that enabled students to bypass developmental courses have been closed. It is somewhat ironic that it was the very existence of these loopholes in the system that made a comparative study of takers and nontakers possible. Finally, it is important to note that the president and board of trustees perceived the issue as significant enough to warrant the allocation of resources to evaluation.

Recent Developments

Since 1979, we have continued to accumulate data on the students who were included in the four-year retrospective study. Our assumption was that the difference in success rates between takers and nontakers as measured by credits earned, grade point averages, and graduation would increase or at least stay the same over time. As of summer 1981, two years after the original study was completed, this assumption continued to be true. As of summer 1981, 51 percent more takers than nontakers had graduated. In addition, takers had a 21 percent higher quality point average and accrued 34 percent more credits.

In the 1981 review of the data, we looked at retention patterns to compare developmental takers with nontakers over a period of four semesters. We found that, of students whose placement test scores indicated a need for developmental English, 94 percent of the takers were retained after one semester, compared with 63 percent of the nontakers. After two semesters, 73 percent of the takers were retained, compared with 38 percent of the nontakers. Overall, it appears that, on the average, 20 percent more takers than nontakers were retained after one, two, and three semesters.

Significant Program Characteristics

Having determined that the developmental studies program contributes effectively both to student success in academic programs and to institutional income, we can describe the characteristics of the developmental studies program that, we believe, contribute to its effectiveness. Two aspects figure prominently: organization and stability.

Organization. Because the developmental studies program is organized as a separate department, developmental faculty and staff are committed full-time to the program. This organization can be contrasted with colleges where responsibility for teaching developmental courses is shared by faculty of several departments.

To accommodate the fact that entering students have different learning needs and rates, the instructional program is organized as a competence-based, individualized program. All students must reach exit competencies, but they do not need to do so in the same time frame. However, students are required to attend regularly and to show progress. Although every effort is made to provide each student with assistance and encouragement, students who do not comply with attendance and assignment requirements are withdrawn from the course.

Organization of the program's physical facilities contributes to its effectiveness. While individual areas of the learning lab are designated for reading, study skills, English, and mathematics, having all developmental instruction in one space facilitates interaction among faculty, students, and counselor. Special attention is given to creating a pleasant environment in which students will feel comfortable and welcome, even after they complete their developmental courses.

Stability. A second important aspect of the developmental studies program is its considerable stability. Since the program is funded by the college budget, it does not depend on external funds to continue. It is unrealistic to assume that stability of a program and its funding has no relationship to effectiveness. Instructors who are insecure in their position and a director whose grantsmanship can determine the future of the program and its staff cannot be as effective as faculty and staff who do not face these concerns. Uncertain funding also negatively affects the essential tasks of planning and developmnt. If one has reason to wonder if a program will exist one year from now, what motivation is there to plan for the next five? Finally, a program that is an integral part of college organization has a positive image and—of particular importance to developmental programs—a certain measure of status. Externally funded programs that provide activities and services for which we have little enthusiasm can be ignored, since it can be assumed that sooner or later they will go away. In shaping faculty and student perceptions, it is important for developmental studies programs not to be viewed in this way.

Conclusion

As a final note on evaluation of program costs and outcomes, we need to acknowledge that program evaluation can be a traumatic experience. Evaluation of the developmental studies at Westmoreland County Community College generated very positive data that were reassuring both to program staff and to the college community. It might have gone the other way. Had that been the case, we would have looked for ways to bring the program in line with student and institutional expectations. If we, as developmental educators, are confident that we can identify and remedy deficiencies in our students, we must be confident that we can identify and remedy deficiencies in our programs.

References

Cicco and Associates. *Westmoreland County Community College Developmental Program Evaluation.* Youngwood, Pa.: Westmoreland County Community College, 1979 (ED 186 053).
Friedlander, J. "An ERIC Review: Should Remediation Be Mandatory?" *Community College Review,* 1981-82, *9* (3), 56-64.

Mary Stubbs is assistant academic dean for learning resources at Westmoreland County Community College, where she has directed the developmental studies program since 1975. She is president of the Pennsylvania Association of Developmental Educators.

Sources of further information are presented in this chapter.

Annotated Bibliography

Lynn B. Burnham

Adult Performance Level Project. *Adult Performance Level Study: Final Report.* Austin: University of Texas, 1977.

This study found that skills in communication, computation, problem solving, and interpersonal relationships account for the majority of skill requirements placed on adults. In order to be functionally competent, an adult must be able to relate and apply the skills just mentioned to the general knowledge areas of occupational knowledge, consumer economics, community resources, government and law, and health. In order to be successful, the adult must achieve a minimum level of competence in all five areas. Under these criteria, approximately one fifth of the adults in the United States are functionally incompetent.

Avila, D. L., Combs, A. W., and Purkey, W. W. *The Helping Relationship Sourcebook.* (2nd ed.) Boston: Allyn & Bacon, 1977.

Chapters in this book are grouped under five heads: The Professional Helper; Psychological Bases for Helping; Beliefs, Values, and Goals in the Helping Process; The Helping Process; and The Person in the Process. Affirming that all behavior is a function of the perceptions existing for any individual at the moment of behaving, the book emphasizes that all helping relationships are essentially learning situations. The last section, The Person in the Process, contains an interesting discussion of continuing intelligence,

J. E. Roueche (Ed.). *A New Look at Successful Programs.* New Directions for College Learning Assistance, no. 11. San Francisco: Jossey-Bass, March 1983.

99

which results when the organism continues to satisfy its needs from life's situations.

Bernstein, A. *Reports from the Fund: Underprepared Students.* Washington, D.C.: Fund for the Improvement of Postsecondary Education, n.d.

This inside view of proposals for underprepared students submitted to the Fund for the Improvement of Postsecondary Education indicates that the strongest proposals are committed to placing underprepared students in a general curriculum while supporting them with specialized teaching techniques. Two new trends are emerging: new ways of counseling students into the world of academe and emphasis on students' learning needs. Total departmental or institutional commitment to remediating skills in a particular academic discipline and evaluating program impact remain problems.

An Evaluative Look at Nontraditional Postsecondary Education. Washington, D.C.: National Institute of Education, 1979.

Prepared by the staff of the Center for Research and Development in Higher Education at the University of California, Berkeley, the three papers in this volume are intended to be a resource for those involved with policy or administration of nontraditional postsecondary education. Topics include analysis of nontraditional population needs and program responses to those needs, kinds of information that decision makers need for nontraditional degree programs, and data and instrumentation that can be used to evaluate nontraditional programs. The quality of writing and clear charts and graphs help to make this volume especially accessible.

Felker, D. W. *Building Positive Self-Concepts.* Minneapolis: Burgess, 1974.

Although this book is perhaps most appealing to teachers of younger students, it contains information, perceptions, and suggestions that can apply to all levels of education. Beginning with the premise that human behavior should be self-controlled, the author analyzes the relationship between sensory data, self-ideas, and self-attitudes. Of particular interest is the discussion of language, which the author views as the central factor in development of self-concept.

Hunter, C., and Harman, D. *Adult Literacy in the United States: A Report to the Ford Foundation.* New York: McGraw-Hill, 1979.

While conceding that there are disparate definitions of illiteracy, this report concentrates on those sixteen years of age and older with less than a high school education, seeing them as severely or partially handicapped in performing everyday tasks required of adults in our society. The report examines categories of representative educational programs designed to combat adult illiteracy and offers general and specific recommendations for action. Its principal overall recommendation is that new, pluralistic, community-based initiatives should be established to serve the most disadvantaged hard-core poor, the bulk of whom never enroll in a program. An extensive annotated bibliography is included.

Klemp. G. O., Jr., Huff, S. M., and Gentile, J. G. *The Guardians of Campus Change: A Study of Leadership in Nontraditional College Programs, Final Report.* Boston: McBer, 1980.

Using behavioral indicators determined empirically from interviews, this study isolates common elements of personality, ability, and style that enable administrators of nontraditional education programs to be successful program leaders. The study thus emphasizes the unique contribution of the program leader to the program's inception and growth over the mechanics of program evolution. An overall observation is that leaders do little or no innovating themselves; they do, however, create a supportive institutional environment within which innovation and change can flourish.

Kozol, J. *Prisoners of Silence.* New York: Continuum, 1980.

The author speaks eloquently of the "somber portraits of the feeling of entrapment which so often overwhelms the man or woman who. . .cannot read or write" (p. 28). Arguing that grade-level performance identifications of literacy are inappropriate for adults, the author reminds us that chances of reaching higher levels of literacy are contingent on prior competence in reading, writing, and basic computation. The key to eliminating illiteracy is teachers—"nonstop, inventive, hard-driving, and determined literacy teachers" (p. 40).

Moore, W., Jr. *Community College Response to the High-Risk Student: A Critical Reappraisal.* Washington, D.C.: American Association of Community and Junior Colleges, 1976.

Contending that the high-risk student has been typecast, Moore attacks the notion of cultural disadvantagement, pointing out that it does not sufficiently consider the effects of school environment, teacher attitude and behavior, poor instruction, validity of standardized test scores, or students' strengths and talents. He argues that institutions must assume more responsibility for improving the performance of high-risk students by emphasizing the principles of andragogy, engaging in thorough academic advising, and recognizing the teacher as the pivotal person in the learning activity. Moore's overriding conclusion is that almost every facet of the community college is in need of in-depth research.

Noel, L. (Ed.). *Reducing the Dropout Rate.* New Directions for Student Services, no. 3. San Francisco: Jossey-Bass, 1978.

The thesis of this sourcebook is simple and direct: Retaining students is a campuswide responsibility. It should not be the goal of an institution but a by-product of better services and programs, which include teaching, counseling, and out-of-class activities. Designed to be a resource for those interested in the specifics of retention activity, the volume addresses related topics, such as admissions management, academic advising, career planning, and steps in starting a campus retention program. Comments by a dean and a president create a rounded perspective. A brief annotated bibliography is included.

Peterson, R. E., and Associates. *Lifelong Learning in America: An Overview of Current Practices, Available Resources, and Future Projects.* San Francisco: Jossey-Bass, 1979.

Written to aid educators in realizing the promise of lifelong learning both locally and throughout the country, the chapters in this book, each by a different educator, discuss adult learners' characteristics, needs, and interests and the study of local needs. Case studies of four states' plans and activities for lifelong learning and a summary of federal programs related to lifelong learning are included. Especially helpful are the guide to resources on lifelong learning and the concluding statement of general implications for planners of lifelong learning.

Roueche, J. E., and Snow, J. J. *Overcoming Learning Problems: A Guide to Developmental Education in College.* San Francisco: Jossey-Bass, 1977.

This book begins with the premise that high-risk students are not limited to minority, disprivileged, or working-class populations; rather, they are found in the entire population. The authors argue that educators must create academic situations in which such students can succeed. They analyze twelve exemplary programs for high-risk students and identify factors related to student improvement and retention. These factors include institutional and degree credit for course work, instructional objectives, criterion-referenced tests, instructors selected for human relations skills, and counselors on the staff.

Roueche, J. E., with Mink, O. G. *Holistic Literacy in College Teaching.* New York: Media Systems, 1980.

This book is based on the premise that education must move away from an emphasis on quantitative and verbal skills and toward an emphasis on holistic learning. This dictates that content, method, environment, and learning style must be addressed equally and simultaneously. Arguing that the curriculum must undergo a values revolution, that student-centered learning means employing subjective evaluation, and that aesthetic-sensory learning is necessary in educating the whole student, the authors stress that the real test of effective education is how well a student uses knowledge when faced with an "ethical dilemma, a real-life problem, or a critical life decision" (p. 37).

Schneider, C., Klemp, G. O., Jr., and Kastendiek, S. *The Balancing Act: Competencies of Effective Teachers and Mentors in Degree Programs for Adults, Final Report.* Chicago: Center for Continuing Education, University of Chicago, and Boston: McBer, 1981.

This study, based on a project supported by the Fund for the Improvement of Postsecondary Education, was designed to generate a competence model that identifies skills, abilities, or characteristics common to superior classroom teaching and mentoring of adult students. What emerges is a profile of the faculty member who acts in ways that enhance the educational experience of the whole student. Key findings are that a dual teaching role of emphasizing the student as a unique individual and of acting in highly directive and prescriptive ways makes a difference to effectiveness over time and that the importance of faculty diagnostic skills has not been sufficiently emphasized in adult education.

Stetson, L. D. "An Assessment of the Attitudes and Opinions of Administrators, Content Faculty, Developmental Faculty, and Students Concerning the Developmental Education Needs of Community College Students." Unpublished doctoral dissertation, Oregon State University, 1979.

Conducted at a community college in the Pacific Northwest, this study found considerable difference of opinion regarding basic skill needs of community college students among the four groups assessed. That difference of opinion extended into operational aspects of the developmental education program. Three of the twelve recommendations made on the basis of data analysis are that reading comprehension, vocabulary, reading rate, and spelling should be considered as a major thrust of developmental education programs in community colleges; a diagnostic testing program prior to registration for classes should be implemented for all entering community college students; and granting college credit for developmental education courses does not appear to be a priority.

Tough, A. *The Adult's Learning Projects.* (2nd ed.) San Diego: University Associates, 1979.

The focus of this book includes only the adult's highly deliberate learning efforts, which are called *learning projects*. Studies reveal that adults participate in an average of five learning projects per year and that they devote 500 hours per year to these projects. Most projects seek established knowledge, gained directly or indirectly from other people who already possess it. Anticipated use or application of the knowledge or skill is the strongest motivation for most learning projects. In relatively few projects is the adult interested in mastering an entire body of subject matter. The author concludes that the amount of appropriate knowledge and skill gained by the typical adult may be even higher in the future than it is now.

Tyler, R. W. *Basic Principles of Curriculum and Instruction.* Chicago: University of Chicago Press, 1949.

The author of this modest but classic treatise emphasizes the importance of educational goals and objectives. Pointing out that objectives become the criteria for selecting materials, outlining content, developing instructional procedures, and preparing examinations, he identifies as sources of objectives the needs of the learner, studies of contemporary life outside the school, subject specialists, educational and social philosophy, and psychology of learning.

Walvekar, C. C. (Ed.). *Assessment of Learning Assistance Services.* New Directions for College Learning Assistance, no. 5. San Francisco: Jossey-Bass, 1981.

Intending to raise awareness of the need for and ways of evaluating learning centers, the nine chapters in this sourcebook address different aspects of that task. The authors discuss limitations of typical evaluation measures and suggest current needs of evaluation, the need to classify types of programs for evaluation purposes, the implications of decision-making evaluation methods, the need to design an evaluation study meticulously, the use of computers in evaluation, how to combine qualitative and quantitative research, and the role of staff performance evaluation in the larger context of program evaluation.

Lynn B. Burnham is a codirector with National Institute for Staff and Organizational Development (NISOD) and editor of Linkages *at the University of Texas, Austin. She has been a curriculum developer, director, instructor, and evaluator in higher education.*

Index